WHAT BELIEVERS DON'T HAVE TO BELIEVE

The Non-Essentials of the Christian Faith

Craig Payne

University Press of America,® Inc.
Lanham · Boulder · New York · Toronto · Oxford

Copyright © 2006 by
University Press of America,® Inc.
4501 Forbes Boulevard
Suite 200
Lanham, Maryland 20706
UPA Acquisitions Department (301) 459-3366

PO Box 317
Oxford
OX2 9RU, UK

Library of Congress Control Number: 2006920085
ISBN-13: 978-0-7618-3426-7 (paperback : alk. paper)
ISBN-10: 0-7618-3426-5 (paperback : alk. paper)

Table of Contents

Introduction: Prolegomena to Any Future Meddling

"Beloved, when I gave all diligence to write unto you of the common salvation, it was needful for me to write unto you, and exhort you that ye should earnestly contend for the faith which was once delivered unto the saints."—Jude 3.

Four Questions

This book is full of questions, with only a few answers. Most of the questions are left for you to answer yourselves. Not only is this a venerable tradition in philosophical discussion—after all, Socrates' questioning style is so well known it even has a title, "the Socratic method"—but it is used as well in the Bible. When the Lord reveals himself to Job, He does so primarily through a series of questions.

Moreover, in the Gospels, it is instructive to count how many times Jesus answers a question with a question: "Who gave you the authority to act as you do?" they ask Him. He replies, "I will answer your question if you answer one of mine: The baptism of John—was it of heavenly origin, or only of men?"[1] His parents ask Him, "Son, why have You thus dealt with us?" He asks them, "Did you not know that I must be about my Father's business?"[2] His enemies seek to trick Him: "Is it lawful for us to pay tribute to Caesar, or not?" He will not be tricked: "Show me a coin. Whose image and superscription is on it?"[3]

Therefore, allow me to begin with a question of my own (actually, four questions).

- Question number one: In your mind, what people count as Christians? Are Protestants Christians? Are Roman Catholics Christians? If people describe themselves as "evangelical" Christians, would that make them more or less likely to be "real" Christians than those who describe themselves as "Eastern Orthodox" Christians? If people describe themselves as "Pentecostal" or "charismatic" Christians, does that make them more or less likely to be "real" Christians than the "evangelicals"? Are Pentecostals and evangelicals for the most part identical in terms of their written statements of faith?

How about Catholics and Orthodox? Are Episcopalians as committed to the Christian faith as are Methodists? Are Methodists as committed as Baptists? If people describe themselves as "born again," does that make them more likely to be "real" Christians than those who say they "confess Christ as Lord"? How about those people who don't use either of those phrases, but who still refer to themselves as Christian?

"These questions are easy enough to answer," you might be thinking. "One's Christian faith doesn't depend on denominational or organizational labels. Anyone can be a Christian as long as . . ."

Yes, that's where the first question is leading. "Anyone can be a Christian as long as"—what, exactly?

You might patiently take me aside at this point and lead me through some scriptures. "Jesus said, 'You must be born again,'" you might explain.[4] "And Paul the apostle spells out the commitment required of us, in the epistle of Romans: We must believe in the sacrifice of Christ for our sins, that Christ has been raised to life again for our justification before God, and we must confess Him as the new Lord of our lives. Whoever does this, confessing Christ as Lord and living under his Lordship, will be saved—will be, in fact, a Christian.[5] It doesn't matter what other label is attached to this person," you might continue. "Real Christianity is of the inner self, the 'hidden man of the heart,'[6] not the outward organization or group. Real Christianity is based on one's relationship with Christ."

To this I would respond: And that's it? You're positive? You're sure about your stance on this? That's what it takes to be a Christian? Believing in Christ's sacrifice, confessing Him as Lord, living under his Lordship?

Assuming that your answer to this question is at least a tentative "Yes," I'll proceed to the second question.

• Let's agree that, if they have responded in faith to Christ as you have described from the Bible, all these different types of Christians under discussion are actually Christians. So here is question number two: Do all these people just discussed count equally in your mind as *Scripture-oriented, Bible-believing Christians?*

Hmm—now that's a different question, isn't it? What is most interesting to me about this question is this: Virtually all of the groups mentioned would maintain that they themselves *are* securely founded in the Bible, and that their beliefs and practices are grounded in God's Word. However, at the same time many of those groups would further maintain that many of the other groups *are not* so founded—that, in fact, many of the others might be Christians in the sense of having Jesus as their Lord, but they are surely second-class Christians (or even third-class) in the sense of not really believing and / or practicing the biblical essentials of the Christian faith.

My thesis in this book is that this stance is unnecessarily divisive, and that it arises for the most part out of an undue emphasis on certain interpretations of the Scriptures. I do not plan to be argumentative or divisive myself (although the reader may judge); rather, I hope to show that many of the biblical interpretations which divide us as fellow Christians are actually extraneous to the essential "bones" of the faith. My hope, in short, is to help heal what I regard as Christian fragmentation without good cause.

This hope leads me to question number three, to be examined more fully in the opening chapter of this book:

- Question number three: How much can one *not believe* and still be a faithful, believing, biblically-oriented Christian? What do believers *not have to* believe? And how much are we *required* to believe?

Again, you might speak up at this point: "It sounds to me like you are trying to water down the Bible's message. You're reaching for a bare-minimum, lowest-common-denominator Christianity. But in my own spiritual life, I want much more than that bare minimum."

Yes, I agree! I agree completely with both your expressed goal of Christian maturity and your spirit of committed Christian discipleship. However, your objection does not directly address the purpose I have in mind. Rather than "lowest-common-denominator" Christianity, I propose to examine what C.S. Lewis calls "mere" Christianity, our "common salvation,"[7] the foundational beliefs of *all* true Christians wherever they may worship.

Of course, this may be more difficult than it sounds. In Lewis's book *Mere Christianity* itself, he points out, "One of the things Christians are disagreed about is the importance of their disagreements":

> When two Christians of different denominations start arguing, it is usually not long before one asks whether such-and-such a point "really matters," and the other replies: "Matter? Why, it's absolutely essential."[8]

I'm sure this objection will arise more than once during the course of your reading of this book, especially as I begin to discuss some of the points of doctrine I say we don't really *have to* believe in order to be faithful, Bible-believing Christians: "What on earth does Payne mean, we don't have to believe this? Why, that teaching is the very foundation-stone of true Christianity!" However, I would ask at least for a fair hearing.

You see, here's the real issue: In both our denominational bodies and personal devotional lives, even if we hold to a number of doctrines and teachings we regard as both biblical and important, which ones are the non-negotiable ones? Which are the teachings that are not only biblical and important, but absolutely essential?

A thought experiment will shed light on what I'm asking. Let us mentally divide other Christians—who might disagree with you on these doctrines and teachings you hold—into two groups: (1) those who are "Christians-with-interpretations-I-regard-as-incorrect"; and (2) those whose interpretations are so far off base they are "Not-really-Christians-at-all."

Have you done the mental division? All right, then:

- Question number four: Let's suppose some people interpreted differently or even denied outright some of the beliefs, doctrines, or teachings you accept as both biblical and important. Which of these beliefs, once denied by these people, would serve in your view to move them from the category of (1) "Christians-with-interpretations-I-regard-as-incorrect," into the category of (2) "Not-really-Christians-at-all"? In other words, what beliefs, if those beliefs were denied or altered by Person A, would move Person A into the category of heretical Christian or even outright non-Christian? And which beliefs would *not* move Person A into either of these categories?

The exploration of these questions will form both the substance of this book and the reason for its existence.

In fact, while we are considering these questions, here's just one more: What do all of the following questions have in common?

- "Did Creation take six literal days?"
- "How old is the Earth? Is it billions of years old, as some say, or only a few thousand years old, as others say?"
- "Are we supposed to read every part of the Bible as equally historical?"
- "Do we have free will or not?"
- "Are humans in a state of 'Total Depravity' or not?"
- "To what political party should we as Christians belong?"
- "Are you voting for [insert any candidate's name]?"
- "Is there going to be a Rapture of the Church? If so, when?"
- "Are we living in the End Times?"

In the spirit of full disclosure, here is my stance throughout the following pages: What all these questions have in common is that *none of them* has a single clear-cut, absolutely essential, biblical answer. Faithful, Bible-believing Christians may differ legitimately over the answers to all of them.

Therefore, it certainly seems that if some beliefs are open to various interpretations by people of sincere faith and scriptural orientation, then using those beliefs as "litmus tests" to gauge another Christian's commitment to Christ, orthodoxy of belief, or understanding of the Bible can only be seen as sectarian and divisive. Although the practice is widespread, our use of these "litmus tests" to judge and classify other Christians on the basis of non-essential doctrines is not only harmful to the unity of the Body of Christ, but damaging to our witness before the world of non-Christians.

If we can look past the differences of gifts, operations, and administrations within Christ's Body—if we can look even further past differences in debatable points of belief—then perhaps we will be better able to see and witness to the same Lord and the same Spirit.[9] I trust that as Christians this vision, this unity, this witness, is our common goal. It is certainly the goal of this book.

Love and Thanks

As we began this Introduction with a quote from the epistle of Jude, let us end with one that expresses my hope for us all: "Now to Him who is able to keep you from stumbling, and to present you faultless before the presence of his glory with exceeding joy, to God our Savior, Who alone is wise, be glory and majesty, dominion and power, both now and forever. Amen."[10]

My sincere thanks first of all to Rhonda Eakins, chair of the Arts and Sciences Department of Indian Hills Community College in southeastern Iowa, where I teach. This book was really her idea in the first place, and, if she had written it, it would be much wiser and more compassionate. Her input and analysis have improved my own efforts greatly. Also, thanks go to her for the title.

Thanks to Pastors Larry and Nancy Ulrich of Family Harvest Church, Agency, Iowa, for their continual patience and guidance over many years. In all areas, their lives are epistles of Christ and revelations of God, written on the tables of the heart.

Thanks to Dr. Lee Wymore for his helpful and continued interest in the topics of Chapter 3; also, thanks to my students of many Bible as Literature classes, especially Joel Minnihan, Rennea Caves, and Andrew Musselman, who kindly prodded me into further thinking on some issues.

Thanks to the journals *De Philosophia* and *Touchstone: A Journal of Ecumenical Orthodoxy*, which published some preliminary articles of mine on subjects addressed in this book.

Thanks to Nathan and Erin, my children, whose Christian faith and walk help keep me humble, grateful, and full of good cheer. And alert.

And thanks to my wife, Desirae, who is a source of perpetual wonder and delight to me. "Let her own works praise her."

Of course, my thanks to these people does not imply that they will agree with everything I have to say in this book. But I do know that even if they do not agree, they will continue to love. My thanks to them for that, as well.

Craig Payne
Ottumwa, Iowa
October 2005

_____

References

1) Luke 20:2-4.

2) Luke 2:48-49.

3) Luke 20:22-24.

4) John 3:7.

5) Romans 10:9-13.

6) 1 Peter 3:4.

7) Jude 3.

8) C.S. Lewis, *Mere Christianity.* 1st paperback edition. New York: Macmillan, 1960: vii.

9) 1 Cor. 12:4-6.

10) Jude 24-25.

Part 1: A Problem and an Answer

Chapter 1: Bones and Bodies

"I'm a Christian, and I don't believe in the Trinity. Are you telling me I'm not a Christian because I don't believe in the Trinity?"—from a former student of mine.

"Well, of course we believe in the Rapture of the Church and the Great Tribulation. We're Bible-believing Christians, and our church teaches the Bible."—from a friend.

Quod semper, quod ubique, quod ab omnibus creditum est. ["What always, what everywhere, what by everyone is believed."]—from Vincent of Lérins, c. A.D. 434.

How Much Is Required?

Teaching in a secular college has taught me as a Christian at least one important lesson: that I should take my comrades in faith where I find them. In the ongoing spiritual, cultural, societal, political, and intellectual wars in which we find ourselves embroiled, our advocacy and defense of Christian beliefs is trying enough without the added difficulty of picking fights with Christians of other doctrinal or liturgical stripes. I have learned to seek what we as Christians hold in common, what unites us, and I've learned not to emphasize unnecessarily what draws us apart.

However, in doing so, the question always looms: What is necessary and what is not? What does it mean to "emphasize unnecessarily" a divisive belief? In my attempt to stress "what unites us" as Christians, have I been guilty of stretching a morsel of agreement farther than it can legitimately be stretched, and so ending up with thin soup indeed? How much can we stress our unity and disregard our differing doctrines without edging into actual compromise of faith?

Many good books exist which set out the basic doctrines of the Christian faith, the teachings we might regard as essential.[1] In this book, I propose something different: to examine what I regard as *non-essentials* of the faith. What is it that divides us unnecessarily? On the other hand, what are the divisions that in fact are necessary? What are the teachings that are non-negotiable, and what are the teachings that we only regard as non-negotiable within our own groups?

Here's another way of asking the same questions: What does it take to be considered a "Bible-believing Christian"? Can one be a biblical Christian and still completely disagree with doctrines that other biblical Christians regard as absolutely crucial for faithful, believing Christianity?

In fact, how much can one *not believe* and still be a faithful, believing, biblically-oriented Christian? What do we *not have to* believe? And how much are we *required* to believe?

Charles Spurgeon, in the *Lectures to His Students*, touches on the delicate balance between negotiation and compromise. All doctrines "which we believe to be true in the Scriptures," he writes, "we shall preach with decision."

> If there be questions which may be regarded as moot, or comparatively unimportant, we shall speak with such a measure of decision about them as may be comely. But points which cannot be moot, which are essential and fundamental, will be declared by us without any stammering, without any inquiring of the people, "What would you wish us to say?" . . . . What we have been taught by God we teach.

However, with virtually his next breath, Spurgeon qualifies this statement:

> How are we to show this decision? . . . . Certainly we are not to show our decision by that obstinate, furious, wolfish bigotry which cuts off every other body from the chance and hope of salvation and the possibility of being regenerate or even decently honest if they happen to differ from us about the color of a scale of the great leviathan. . . . Do not go about the world with your fist doubled up for fighting, carrying a theological revolver in the leg of your trousers.[2]

Probably all of us have encountered a fellow believer or two packing a "theological revolver." Perhaps even we ourselves may have been a bit quick on the theological draw at times. Religious beliefs, after all, are definitely topics that lead to heated discussions—which is precisely why many people avoid "religious" conversations.

However, even though temperamentally we might not enjoy the conflict, isn't it *right* to stand up for our beliefs? What counts as a legitimate doctrinal defense and what counts as, in Spurgeon's phrase, a dispute over the "color of a scale of the great leviathan"? What is "moot, or comparatively unimportant," again in Spurgeon's words?

Consider this analogy. We refer to our local church congregations as "bodies" of believers, and rightly so, since we are instructed by Scripture to consider ourselves as an organic unity: "Now ye are the body of Christ, and members in particular."[3] However, I'd like to extend the metaphor a bit. We all have local "bodies" of fellowship, belief, and practice. Over here is a Baptist "body," and over here a Pentecostal "body." Over here are the Catholics, here the Orthodox, here the Methodist, and here the Lutheran. We could go on indefinitely, listing all the various Christian "bodies."

But what are the "bones" of these bodies? Probably a Pentecostal would not feel at home in a Church of Christ service, and vice versa. Probably a Baptist would not receive the full benefit from a Catholic mass, nor a Catholic from a Methodist youth meeting. But what do they all have in common? What makes them all refer to themselves as "Christian"?

When we strip away the outward observances (even though the practitioners of those observances certainly and rightly prize them), when we strip down to the bare "bones"—what is it that we find? What do we have left that is absolutely fundamental to regarding ourselves as Christians? What are the important bones under our various bodies?

Questions for Reflection:

1. As we turn to the next section, I'm going to make use of the quotations at the beginning of this chapter, one of which is from Vincent of Lérins. Are you more inclined to trust Vincent, as an early fifth-century Roman Catholic church father, or Charles Spurgeon, the great Calvinist Protestant minister of the 1800s just discussed? Why?

2. In your personal Christian stance, are you inclined to trust neither Vincent nor Spurgeon? Why or why not?

3. If Vincent and Spurgeon had traveled through time and met each other, do you think they would have accepted each other as fellow Christians? Or would neither one have believed the other was "saved"? Why do you think this?

Vincent's Guideline: Universality, Antiquity, Consent

In his work *A Commonitory*, written around A.D. 434, Vincent of Lérins, an early Roman Catholic church father, addresses the question *What is Christianity? What do Christians believe and teach?* Before addressing this question, he points out that it is not enough simply to reply, "We believe and teach the Bible, the Word of God." Virtually all Christian groups would say the same. However, even though commonly presented as a sufficient response, that answer still allows for, as Vincent puts it, "great intricacies of such various error." He states the problem:

> Owing to the depth of Holy Scripture, all do not accept it in one and the same sense, but one understands its words in one way, another in another; so that it seems to be capable of as many interpretations as there are interpreters. For Novatian expounds it one way, Sabellius another,

Donatus another, Arius, Eunomius, Macedonius, another, Photinus, Apollinaris, Priscillian, another, Iovinian, Pelagius, Celestius, another, lastly, Nestorius another.[4]

As we can readily see, the problem of sectarianism is not a new one. Probably all of these commentators on Scripture had their theological revolvers (or theological swords) tucked away securely under their robes. And all of them would maintain that they taught the Word of God as presented in the Bible. (In fact, it is ironic that Vincent of Lérins himself has been suspected by some writers of semi-heretical sympathies, although in general his views are close to those of mainstream Eastern Orthodoxy.) So, since such a multitude of interpretations exists, what are the "bones" of Christian teaching? What is it that all Christians, of whatever variety, should hold to as a standard of faith?

Vincent's answer is still today regarded as both classic and admirably succinct:

> Moreover, in the Catholic Church itself, all possible care must be taken, that we hold that faith which has been believed everywhere, always, by all. For that is truly and in the strictest sense "Catholic" [universal], which, as the name itself and the reason of the thing declare, comprehends all universally. This rule we shall observe if we follow universality, antiquity, consent.[5]

This short passage is usually shortened to the even shorter and simpler "What always, what everywhere, what by everyone has been believed." Thus Vincent answers the question: What is basic Christian teaching? It is, according to this guideline, only that which satisfies the following:

- *It is universal.* It is not a teaching peculiar to North America, Russia, Kenya, New Zealand, or any other specific area. It is a teaching accepted by Christians world-wide.

- *It has existed from antiquity.* In other words, it has been a Christian teaching, at least in a rudimentary form, since the beginning of the Christian church.

- *It has the consent of the church.* The *majority* of Christians, world-wide, throughout history, has accepted it.

Here we reach the bones under the various bodies of denominational Christianity. Would not most Christians embrace all beliefs satisfying these basic standards, even if they then went on to embrace much more in their doctrinal commitments? Some bodies of belief contain a great deal more than other bodies of belief, but at least they all contain an inner core of teachings seen as universally accepted, from antiquity, by common consent.

Questions for Reflection:

1. As you consider the doctrines that you know of within Christian teaching, how many of them would you judge as having been believed by the majority of Christians world-wide throughout the entire history of Christianity?

2. At the beginning of this chapter, I quoted a friend of mine, from a recent conversation: "Well, of course we believe in the Rapture of the Church and the Great Tribulation. We're Bible-believing Christians, and our church teaches the Bible." How might Vincent's guideline apply to this statement? How might it be used by someone defending the doctrine of the Rapture of the Church as fundamental and binding? How might it be used by someone opposing the same doctrine?

3. The following is from Vincent, quoted earlier: "Moreover, in the Catholic Church itself, all possible care must be taken, that we hold that faith which has been believed everywhere, always, by all. For that is truly and in the strictest sense 'Catholic,' which, as the name itself and the reason of the thing declare, comprehends all universally." When you read Vincent's term "the Catholic Church itself," do you think he means the universal body of Christ, or does he mean the Roman Catholic Church in particular? What does he mean by saying that the Church "comprehends all universally"?

The Guideline in Action

I lean heavily on Vincent's response in many of the college classes I teach. These classes include what is usually called the "humanities": classes in literature, for example, religion and philosophy, ethics and intellectual history, and so on. I also teach a course called "The Bible as Literature" which usually draws an astonishing range of students—all the way from retired or active Christian ministers to people who honestly have never heard that there are such things as "Old" and "New" Testaments.

In these courses, I sometimes casually refer to "what Christians believe" or "what Jews believe" or "what the Bible teaches" or, conversely, "what the Bible doesn't teach." One might think these phrases betray a "know-it-all" attitude regarding biblical and Christian teaching. However, such an attitude has never really had a chance to take root, especially since my students are remarkably quick to challenge me whenever these phrases are used:

- "What do you mean, 'what Christians believe'? Christians believe all sorts of things. Are you the final authority on Christian belief?"

- "I grew up in my parents' church, and I know they don't believe what you say the Bible teaches. But they believe the Bible, too. Why is your interpretation any better than theirs?"

- "Since Christianity is so hopelessly divided, how can you say there is such a thing as 'what Christians believe'? For every doctrine you mention, I'll bet we could find Christians who don't believe it."

When these questions arise, Vincent's guideline always is my first response. Here is an example of how this guideline has been helpful in clarifying problems and reaching understanding, not only for me, but also for those with whom I am in disagreement:

While lecturing in a class on medieval philosophy, I referred to the medieval view of the complementarity of *fides et ratio*, faith and reason, reaffirmed in the twentieth century by Pope John Paul II. "For example," I said, "Thomas Aquinas, the greatest of medieval philosophers, believed that we could demonstrate the *existence* of God by reason, but faith is required to know that God is a Trinity. You can know logically that God exists, Aquinas thought, but to know God as a Trinity, you have to accept by faith what Christianity teaches. Faith does not contradict reason, but does reach beyond it." A perfectly fine example, I thought, and continued on to something else.

But not for long. Suddenly a young woman spoke out, with barely disguised fury: "I'm a Christian, and I don't believe in the Trinity. Are you telling me I'm not a Christian because I don't believe in the Trinity?"

The class was taken aback at the outburst. "Well, no," I said. "I'm using an example to illustrate the distinction between knowing something by faith and knowing it by logic." I went on to explain further—well enough, I thought, to maintain my own equilibrium. But at that point another student spoke up, equally vehemently. His comment was not directed at me, but at the first student: "If you don't believe the *whole* Bible," he said, "you are *not* a Christian!" A general babble erupted.

At least the other students were witnessing the give-and-take of ideas. For some, the concept of the Trinity was as non-controversial as apple pie. For others, this may have been the first time they'd ever seriously thought about it. Some were frankly puzzled at the seriousness with which the students were arguing. Many of them looked at me questioningly: *So what do you say now?* I suppose at this point maintaining my own equilibrium was no longer my primary concern.

If you ever find yourself in such a situation—where anything you say on either side seems bound to offend—I recommend falling back on Vincent's guideline. "Let's not discuss our personal interpretations of the Bible right now," I said, "or how much of the Bible we accept or believe. Instead, let's discuss the *Christian* interpretation of the Bible."

Some of the class looked at me with frowns, some with relief, but most with puzzlement. I explained Vincent's statement and applied it to the subject under discussion: "*Quod semper*—have Christians taught that God is a Trinity throughout the entire history of Christianity, from antiquity?" Most students— even the young woman who didn't believe in the Trinity—agreed. "*Quod ubique*—has this been a world-wide, universal teaching?" Again, most agreed. "*Quod ab omnibus*—has it been believed by the *majority* of Christians throughout Christian history? Has it obtained majority consent?"

The students began to see the point, but I spelled it out. "This is one good way to judge what is or is not standard Christian teaching. The teaching that God is a Trinity satisfies all three of these requirements.

"So, no matter what your church teaches (and I'm not arguing whether your church is right or wrong), and no matter what you personally may believe (and again, I'm not arguing whether you are right or wrong), the *fundamental Christian teaching* is that God is a Trinity. You certainly are free to reject that teaching—as long as you recognize in doing so that you are rejecting what the majority of Christians have always believed and taught."

This point can't be emphasized enough to most people discussing religion in general, and Christianity in particular: *Christianity has objective teachings.* You can't believe just anything at all you want to believe and call it Christian. Though your relationship with God may be "personal," your relationship with the fundamental teachings of the Christian faith depends heavily on what Christians historically have defined as those fundamental teachings. Vincent refers to this as "the consentient definitions and determinations of all."[6] (By the way, the young woman in this classroom discussion has since become both a friend *and* a Christian; she tells me she realizes now that she was not really a Christian at the time she asked the initial question. In fact, it was partially this very discussion that led her to question herself and her own relationship with Christ.)

On the other hand, let's move now out of the classroom and into our relationships with fellow Christians. Granted that Christianity has objectively existing beliefs, and granted that some of these beliefs are primary and fundamental, the question still remains with us: Exactly *what beliefs* are important enough to warrant the breaking of fellowship or the denial of someone else's orthodoxy? Earlier I asked, "What are the teachings that are non-negotiable, and what are the teachings that we only regard as non-negotiable within our own groups?" I would like to suggest that Vincent's guideline serves as a useful touchstone in this area as well.

Let us regard as non-negotiable whatever has been accepted (1) by the *consent* of the majority of Christians [*quod ab omnibus*], (2) *universally* world-wide [*quod ubique*], and (3) throughout the entire history of Christianity from *antiquity* [*quod semper*]. Anything else in our teaching is probably a matter of localized biblical interpretation, not a matter of primary and fundamental beliefs. Further, please note carefully: I am not saying these localized biblical interpretations necessarily are *wrong*. However, I am saying they are not to be used as a litmus test for orthodoxy or for continued fellowship with Christians who do not accept them.

Discovering the non-negotiable in our faith will require a closer look at the early creeds of the Christian church, to be taken up in the next chapter. What did the earliest Christians regard as crucial and binding? What has the majority accepted as "the consentient definitions and determinations of all"? And I think we may be surprised to find how many, how very many, of our favorite teachings are actually extraneous to the "bones" of Christian belief.

Questions for Reflection:

1. Try to apply Vincent's guideline to some of the beliefs you yourself hold. How well do they stand up?

2. After reading the first chapter, can you tell whether the author considers himself Roman Catholic, Eastern Orthodox, or Protestant? Would the answer make a difference in your decision whether or not to read further?

References

1) For example, C.S. Lewis's *Mere Christianity*; John Stott's *Basic Christianity*; P.C. Nelson's *Bible Doctrines*; Joseph Ratzinger's *Introduction to Christianity*; and so on. More recently, *One Faith: The Evangelical Consensus*, edited by J. Packer and Thomas C. Oden, is also good, and affirms historic creedal statements within the context of evangelicalism.

2) Charles Spurgeon, *Spurgeon's Lectures to His Students*. Edited by David Otis Fuller. 3rd edition. Grand Rapids: Zondervan, 1945: 212-213.

3) 1 Corinthians 12:27. Other scriptural passages could be multiplied on this point.

4) Vincent of Lérins, *A Commonitory*. Trans. by C.A. Heurtley. *Nicene and Post-Nicene Fathers, Volume Eleven*. Edited by Philip Schaff and Henry Wace. 2nd series. 4th printing. Peabody, Mass.: Hendrickson Publishers, 2004: 132.

5) *A Commonitory*, p. 132.

6) *A Commonitory*, p. 132.

Chapter 2: "Living Tradition" or Living Tradition?

"Creed: A creed is a concise, formal, and authorized statement of important points of Christian doctrine, the classical instances being the Apostles' Creed and the Nicene Creed."—from *The Oxford Dictionary of the Christian Church*.[1]

"Now, with regard to this rule of faith [the creed] .... This rule, as it will be proved, was taught by Christ, and raises amongst ourselves no other questions than those which heresies introduce, and which make men heretics."—from Tertullian, c. A.D. 200.

Creeds, the Church, and the Bible

In the first chapter, the following question was raised: When we strip down to the bare "bones" under our congregational and denominational "bodies," what is it that we find? What do we have left that is absolutely fundamental to regarding ourselves as Christians? What are the important bones under our various bodies? In seeking to answer this question, I referred to the work of Vincent of Lérins, in particular his idea that any basic Christian teaching, in order to deserve the adjective "basic," should satisfy the tests of universality, antiquity, and consent.

In this chapter, I would like us to explore the most obvious teachings which most Christians would agree meet the challenge of these three tests: the Christian creedal statements.

Perhaps not many Christians find creedal statements very interesting. For instance, C.S. Lewis records a conversation held between himself and an elderly military officer. Lewis had just finished giving a lecture defending the Christian faith to a group of Royal Air Force members. His experience and the lesson he drew from it are worth recording at some length:

> In a way I quite understand why some people are put off by Theology. I remember once when I had been giving a talk to the R.A.F., an old, hard-bitten officer got up and said, "I've no use for all that stuff. But, mind you, I'm a religious man too. I *know* there's a God. I've *felt* Him: out alone in the desert at night: the tremendous mystery. And that's just why I don't

believe all your neat little dogmas and formulas about Him. To anyone who's met the real thing they all seem so petty and pedantic and unreal!"

Now in a sense I quite agreed with that man. I think he had probably had a real experience of God in the desert. And when he turned from that experience to the Christian creeds, I think he really was turning from something real to something *less* real. In the same way, if a man has once looked at the Atlantic from the beach, and then goes and looks at a map of the Atlantic, he also will be turning from something real to something less real: turning from real waves to a bit of coloured paper. . . .

Now, Theology is like the map. Merely learning and thinking about the Christian doctrines, if you stop there, is less real and less exciting than the sort of thing my friend got in the desert. Doctrines are not God: they are only a kind of map. But that map is based on the experience of hundreds of people who really were in touch with God—experiences compared with which any thrills or pious feelings you and I are likely to get on our own are very elementary and very confused. And secondly, if you want to get any further, you must use the map.[2]

Lewis's point regarding the necessity of theology in general applies also to the necessity of the particular theological declarations known as "creeds." You may be a believer who finds little use for creeds, or who finds them too "liturgical" for your own church's worship style. However, these creeds do serve to delineate the "bones" undergirding our local "bodies," even if we do not refer to them often, or at all. They are the "map"; and, although the map is not as interesting as the actual scenery, it does tend to keep us on the right road.

In Latin, the *lingua franca* of early Christianity as it spread from the Middle East throughout Europe, the word *credo* simply means "I believe." Formal creedal statements begin with this word (e.g., *Credo in Deum Patrem*, "I believe in God the Father"), and the word "creed" itself is derived from *credo*. The most popular and well known of these creeds are the Apostles' Creed, the Nicene Creed (most often used in Eastern Orthodox services), and, less well known and less frequently used, the Athanasian Creed. The complete texts of these creeds are contained in this chapter's footnotes.[3]

According to Stuart Briscoe in his book *The Apostles' Creed*, there were three primary reasons for the development of formal creeds:

- To give a powerful statement of orthodox Christian belief.

- To address specific heretical incursions in Christian thinking. (The term "heretic," as opposed to "heathen" or "unbeliever," refers to one who retains the name of Christian while formally denying fundamental doctrines of Christianity.)

- To aid Christians in making a clearer statement of their faith, in order that they might confess what they truly believed.[4]

In addition to these three reasons for their development, these creeds served four specific functions in the practices of early Christians. They were used in baptismal services, for instance:

> The creed developed as a baptismal formula. The most important is the Roman symbol which underwent various revisions until the seventh century, and came finally to be known as "The Apostles' Creed." [To this creed] the baptized yielded assent on their immersion.[5]

The creeds were also used for instructional purposes, as a sort of rudimentary catechism. Thirdly, creeds had a liturgical significance, as they were incorporated into Christian worship services, especially those revolving around the Lord's Supper. Finally, the creeds served a doctrinal function, a standard of orthodoxy by which to gauge heretical variations.[6]

In fact, in his work *The Prescription Against Heretics* (c. A.D. 200), the great North African church father Tertullian summarized an early creed as a guideline by which to detect heresy:

> Now, with regard to this rule of faith—that we may from this point acknowledge what it is which we defend—it is, you must know, that which prescribes the belief that there is one only God, and that He is none other than the Creator of the world, who produced all things out of nothing through His own Word, first of all sent forth; that this Word is called His Son, and, under the name of God, was seen "in diverse manners" by the patriarchs, heard at all times in the prophets, at last brought down by the Spirit and Power of the Father into the Virgin Mary, was made flesh in her womb, and, being born of her, went forth as Jesus Christ; thenceforth He preached the new law and the new promise of the kingdom of heaven, worked miracles; having been crucified, He rose again the third day; (then) having ascended into the heavens, He sat at the right hand of the Father; sent instead of Himself the Power of the Holy Ghost to lead such as believe; will come with glory to take the saints to the enjoyment of everlasting life and of the heavenly promises, and to condemn the wicked to everlasting fire, after the resurrection of both these classes shall have happened, together with the restoration of their flesh. This rule, as it will be proved, was taught by Christ, and raises amongst ourselves no other questions than those which heresies introduce, and which make men heretics.[7]

This passage so closely parallels the creedal statements finalized many years later, it must certainly be based on an early form of the same statements.

However, even before these more formal statements were established and accepted, the New Testament itself contained numerous creedal formulations and ideas which eventually were used in the later creeds. To give just three examples, the following scriptural passages are often cited by scholars as probable confessional statements, either repeated by new converts at baptism or held by believers as an easily memorized way of maintaining orthodoxy:

Yet for us there is but one God, the Father, from whom are all things and for whom we exist, and one Lord, Jesus Christ, through whom are all things and through whom we exist.[8]

For I delivered to you as of first importance what I also received, that Christ died for our sins in accordance with the scriptures, that He was buried, that He was raised on the third day in accordance with the scriptures, and that He appeared to Cephas, then to the twelve. Then He appeared to more than five hundred brethren at one time, most of whom are still alive, though some have fallen asleep. Then He appeared to James, then to all the apostles.[9]

And without controversy, great is the mystery of godliness: God was manifest in the flesh, justified in the Spirit, seen of angels, preached unto the Gentiles, believed on in the world, received up into glory.[10]

Notice the themes stressed as crucial by Paul (as well as other New Testament writers): the Incarnation ("God was manifest in the flesh"); God and Christ as co-creators (and thus equal in divinity and divine activity); the reality of the Resurrection; and so on. These are the same themes, in short, we find stressed in the creeds.

So, although the creeds are neither inspired nor authoritative in the same way as the New Testament, still they are firmly rooted in the teachings of Scripture and legitimized by the common consent of the overwhelming voice of Christian believers through the centuries. They codify the elements of Christian faith which satisfy Vincent's tests of universality, antiquity, and consent. They are a standard of orthodoxy, part of the living tradition that both roots us in the past and points us toward our future.

Questions for Reflection:

1. Review Stuart Briscoe's three primary reasons for the development of creeds. In the contemporary Christian Church, how well do you think these creeds fulfill their reasons for existence?

2. Many non-liturgical churches (Pentecostal and evangelical churches, in particular) do not recite the creeds in services, or otherwise refer to them in any way. Are there good reasons for this? What are they?

3. I mentioned that the creeds are not "authoritative" in the same way the Scriptures are authoritative. Do you regard them as authoritative in any other way? In what way?

Roman Catholicism and the "Development of Doctrine"

At this point, although I'd like to continue in the exposition of the creeds themselves, it seems to me a slight digression is necessary, in order to bring up and discuss an extensive and continuing disagreement between Roman Catholic Christians on the one hand, and Protestant and Eastern Orthodox Christians on the other. This disagreement revolves around the nature of the "living tradition" of Christianity. In particular, the disagreement is over the process of the "development of doctrine" within the Roman Catholic Church.

When I use the phrase "development of doctrine," I have especially in mind John Henry Cardinal Newman's definition of and defense of those words, in his *Essay on the Development of Christian Doctrine*. Regarding this "development" he writes, "The question is this: whether there was not from the first a certain element at work, or in existence, divinely sanctioned, which, for certain reasons, did not at once show itself upon the surface of ecclesiastical affairs."[11]

Behind this quote lie numerous doctrinal issues and problems. If we adopt Vincent of Lérins' guidelines of universality, antiquity, and consent, many teachings of the Roman Catholic Church appear to violate those guidelines, since they were not accepted by the majority of Christians world-wide, and especially not from antiquity, since both the Bible and the early church fathers appear silent regarding them. Such doctrines would include the Assumption of Mary, the Immaculate Conception of Mary, the idea of papal supremacy, and so on. So Newman argues for a "development" of doctrine—that there was "from the first a certain element at work, or in existence," which would validate these teachings even from the earliest years of Christianity, but which was not explicitly spelled out until the later "ecclesiastical affairs" of the Roman Catholic Church brought it to light.

Vincent of Lérins himself allows for the expansion of understanding in doctrinal issues: "But some one will say, perhaps, Shall there then be no progress in Christ's Church? Certainly; all possible progress. . . . Yet on condition that it be real progress, not alteration of the faith." He distinguishes between "progress" and "alteration": "For progress requires that the subject be enlarged in itself, alteration, that it be transformed into something else."[12]

However, Newman argues that progress and alteration are not always easily distinguished. The oak tree is not easily perceived in the acorn, yet the one does undeniably arise out of the other; as one Catholic apologist writes, "The oak tree has grown and looks perceptibly different from the fragile sprout that cracked the original acorn, yet the organic essence and identity remain the same."[13] In Newman's view, this analogy illustrates the relation of the current Catholic Church (the oak) to the biblical and patristic writings (the acorn), and so Vincent's guidelines of orthodoxy cannot readily be used today:

> True as the dictum of Vincentius must be considered in the abstract, and possible as its application might be in his own age, when he might

almost ask the primitive centuries for their testimony, it is hardly available
now, or effective of any satisfactory result.[14]

We are faced, therefore, with two questions regarding the "development of
doctrine" within the Catholic Church: (1) Is it or is it not a true "development," a
"progress" of understanding which was implicit in the earlier stated doctrines
themselves, as the oak is implicit in the acorn? Is it part of the "living tradition"
of the living Church, the voice of the Spirit in our historical development? Or is
it an "alteration," something completely new and unprecedented with no
patristic authority, no "organic essence and identity"? Is it truly a "living
tradition," or is it rather an inorganic appendage on the really living tradition of
the biblical writings and creedal statements?

Secondly, if there has been in fact an expansion of understanding of basic
doctrines in the Catholic Church: (2) At what point in the "expansion" do these
expanded teachings become binding only on Catholics, not on non-Catholic
Christians? Or—even if we grant that the voice of the Spirit is being expressed
in the "development of doctrine" in the Catholic Church—does that necessarily
mean the doctrines so developed must also be accepted by Protestant and
Orthodox Christians?

These two groups (Protestant and Orthodox) criticize the "development of
doctrine" notion on many fronts. For example, they often claim that it is a type
of supercessionism, in which doctrines arising chronologically later in
Catholicism take precedence over the earlier writings. As one Orthodox theologian puts it, the patristic church councils "defined everything that needed
defining," but then Catholicism "kept on defining."[15]

On the other hand, Newman argues[16] that if non-Roman Catholic Christians
do not accept the "development of doctrine" concept, they should also not
accept the Athanasian Creed, which arose at roughly the same time as some of
the Catholic teachings being disputed. However, Protestants typically respond
that the Trinitarian assertions of the Athanasian Creed have a much longer and
more explicit history than assertions of these other disputed teachings. Patristic
writers (non-New Testament) refer to Jesus as God as early as A.D. 100.
Furthermore, the New Testament certainly contains many more passages
regarding the divinity both of Christ and of the Holy Spirit—and these passages
are much more amenable to acceptance by non-Catholics—than it contains
passages about, for example, papal supremacy or Mary's Assumption. To accept
these latter teachings, one must not only accept the authority of the Bible and the
creeds; one must accept the teaching authority of the Roman Catholic Church as
binding upon *all* Christians. This seems to lead to circular reasoning: "Why
should we accept the teaching authority of the Catholic Church as binding upon
all Christians?" "Because under the supervision of the Holy Spirit, the development of doctrine takes place within the Catholic Church." "And why should we
accept the idea of a Catholic 'development of doctrine'?" "Because the teaching
authority possessed by the Catholic Church is binding upon all Christians."

In the book *Roman Catholics and Evangelicals: Agreements and Differences*, the two basic Protestant criticisms are stated succinctly:

> Evangelicals may critique Newman's development model at several points: first, his identification of the Roman jurisdiction as being *the* authentic, "true" church, and second, his use of his theory to develop dogmas (i.e., concerning the virgin Mary, the sacraments, etc.), which are rejected by non-Roman Catholic Christians.[17]

Catholics rightly point back to Vincent's dictum that "progress requires that the subject be enlarged in itself." They argue that, in order for the Church truly to possess a "living" tradition, the tradition must be capable of being modified, even greatly modified (without radical "alteration" of its essence). However, the evangelical objection still stands, that Protestants and Orthodox do not accept the Roman Catholic Church as "the" Church whose modifications of teaching are "the" modifications that must be accepted by all Christians. Further, evangelicals also point out that Vincent's original intention (as discussed in Chapter 1 of this book) was to guide the interpretation of *Scripture* in the Christian church *universally*; his intention was not necessarily to write a "blank check" for the expansion of teachings or refinement of tradition within the Roman Catholic Church alone.

In other words, Newman is only partially correct: In order to be a believing and faithful Roman Catholic Christian, one should accept the teaching authority, and the expansion of teachings, of the Roman Catholic Church. However, that acceptance is not necessary in order for one to be an orthodox and faithful "mere" Christian. Being sovereign, God works in history through all those serving Him; therefore, all Christians should be able to reach some level of agreement as to the core, the "mere Christianity," that truly is necessary for all to accept.

As examples of what's necessary, we'll turn away from this discussion and return now to the creeds.

Questions for Reflection:

1. If you are a Roman Catholic, do you think that the teachings of the Roman Catholic Church are binding, or should be binding, upon all Christians?

2. If you are a Roman Catholic, how do you react to the Protestant or Orthodox charge that Catholicism has "altered" biblical teachings rather than "expanded" them?

3. If you are not a Roman Catholic, who or what do you regard as a "teaching authority" to guide the Christian Church?

4.   If you are not a Roman Catholic, and your answer to Question 3 is, "Our teaching authority is the plain sense of the Bible," or, "Our teaching authority is the guidance of the Holy Spirit," how do you respond to the argument of Vincent of Lérins, quoted in Chapter 1, that the Bible has such a multitudinous variety of interpreters and interpretations it requires guidelines for interpretation rooted in the traditional teachings of the Church?

5.   Do you think the worship services and teachings of most Christian churches are more like or more unlike each other? Why do you think this?

6.   Do you have any Roman Catholic friends you consider to be committed Christians? Protestant friends? Eastern Orthodox friends?

The Statements of Faith

We return to the examination of the bones under our various bodies. What counts as doctrines all Christians do or should believe?

To respond to that question, I'd like to present the basic teachings of the three creeds we've been using as examples, by dividing them up and placing their relevant sections next to each other. These are the teachings comprising the Apostles' Creed (hereafter referred to as AC), the Nicene Creed (NC), and the Athanasian Creed (AthC). I'll place my own summary statement at the beginning of these sections of the creeds, and also place supporting scriptures in footnotes; these will not, of course, be all the scriptures the Bible contains on these teachings, but only a small representative sampling.

Here are the creedal statements:

- God exists.[18]

I believe in God the Father almighty . . . (AC)
I believe in one God the Father Almighty . . . (NC)
We worship one God . . . (AthC)

- All other really existing things exist because God caused them to exist. He is the Creator.[19]

Maker of heaven and earth . . . (AC)
Maker of heaven and earth, and of all things visible and invisible. (NC)

- Jesus is the Son of God, God manifest in flesh, made human in the Virgin Mary by the Holy Spirit.[20]

And in Jesus Christ his only Son, our Lord; who was conceived by the Holy Spirit, born of the Virgin Mary . . . (AC)
And in one Lord Jesus Christ, the only-begotten Son of God, begotten of the Father before all worlds, God of God, Light of Light, very God of very God, begotten, not made, being of one substance with the Father; by whom all things were made; who, for us men and for our salvation, came down from heaven, and was incarnate by the Holy Spirit of the Virgin Mary, and was made man . . . (NC)

- Jesus lived at a certain time in history, was crucified, rose again from the dead, and ascended into heaven.[21]

Suffered under Pontius Pilate, was crucified, dead, and buried; He descended into hell; the third day He rose again from the dead; He ascended into heaven, and sitteth on the right hand of God the Father almighty . . . (AC)
And was crucified also for us under Pontius Pilate; He suffered and was buried; and the third day He rose again, according to the Scriptures; and ascended into heaven, and sitteth on the right hand of the Father . . . (NC)

- Jesus shall judge all humanity and rule as Lord forever.[22]

From thence He shall come to judge the living and the dead. (AC)
And He shall come again, with glory, to judge both the living and the dead; whose kingdom shall have no end. (NC)

- The Holy Spirit also is God, the third Person of the Trinity.[23]

I believe in the Holy Spirit . . . (AC)
And I believe in the Holy Spirit, the Lord and Giver of life; who proceedeth from the Father and the Son; who with the Father and the Son together is worshipped and glorified; who spoke by the prophets. (NC)
[We worship one God] in trinity, and trinity in unity, neither confounding the Persons nor dividing the substance. For the Person of the Father is one; of the Son, another; of the Holy Spirit, another. But the divinity of the Father and of the Son and of the Holy Spirit is one, the glory equal, the majesty equal. Such as is the Father, such also is the Son, and such the Holy Spirit. The Father is uncreated, the Son is uncreated, the Holy Spirit is uncreated. The Father is infinite, the Son is infinite, the Holy Spirit is infinite. The Father is eternal, the Son is eternal, the Holy Spirit is eternal. And yet there are not three eternal Beings, but one eternal Being. So also there are not three uncreated Beings, nor three infinite Beings, but one uncreated and one infinite Being. In like manner, the Father is omnipotent, the Son is omnipotent, and the Holy Spirit is omnipotent. And yet there are not three omnipotent Beings, but one omnipotent Being. Thus the Father is God, the Son is God, and the Holy Spirit is God. And yet there are not three Gods, but one God only. The Father is Lord, the Son is Lord, and the Holy Spirit is Lord. And yet there are not three Lords, but one Lord only. For as we are compelled by Christian truth to confess each person distinctively to be both God and Lord, we are prohibited by the Catholic religion to say that there are three Gods or Lords. The Father is made by none, nor created, nor begotten. The Son is from the Father alone, not made, not created, but begotten. The Holy Spirit is not created by the Father and the Son, nor begotten, but proceeds. Therefore, there is one Father, not three Fathers; one Son, not three Sons; one

Holy Spirit, not three Holy Spirits. And in this Trinity there is nothing prior or posterior, nothing greater or less, but all three persons are coeternal and coequal to themselves. So that through all, as was said above, both unity in trinity and trinity in unity is to be adored. Whoever would be saved, let him think thus concerning the Trinity. (AthC)

- There is truly only one spiritual Church, made up of all faithful in Christ, those who have received the forgiveness of sins offered to all. (The word "Catholic" used throughout the creeds comes from the Greek *katholikos*, "universal" or "throughout the whole." It is not to be taken as referring specifically to the Roman Catholic Church.)[24]

[I believe in] the holy catholic church; the communion of saints; the forgiveness of sins. (AC)
And I believe in one holy catholic and apostolic church. I acknowledge one baptism for the remission of sins . . . (NC)

- There will be a final resurrection of the body and eternal blessedness with God in heaven.[25]

[T]he resurrection of the body; and the life everlasting. Amen. (AC)
[A]nd I look for the resurrection of the dead, and the life of the world to come. Amen. (NC)

"Amen" indeed, to all of the above.
Now I realize that my summary statements are a simplified version of the already straightforward creeds:

God exists.
All other really existing things exist because God caused them to exist. He is the Creator.
Jesus is the Son of God, God manifest in flesh, made human in the Virgin Mary by the Holy Spirit.
Jesus lived at a certain time in history, was crucified, rose again from the dead, and ascended into heaven.
Jesus shall judge all humanity and rule as Lord forever.
The Holy Spirit also is God, the third Person of the Trinity.
There is truly only one spiritual Church, made up of all faithful in Christ, those who have received the forgiveness of sins offered to all.
There will be a final resurrection of the body and eternal blessedness with God in heaven.

In fact, you may think that, as a presentation of Christian beliefs, these summary statements are overly simplified. However, in today's extraordinarily secularized environment, we can no longer assume even basic familiarity with Christian teachings on the part of our hearers. Most of my students receive most of their impressions of Christians, Christian history, and Christian beliefs from the parodies and mockeries they see on television and in the movies. Therefore, when I am dealing with those who know little or nothing about Christianity, such as those with honest questions in a secular college classroom, I boil down the necessary teachings even further, to only three elements:

- Christians believe that God has revealed Himself as a Trinity, God the Father, God the Son, and God the Holy Spirit, one God in three Persons.

- Christians believe that God the Son became human and was named Jesus, simultaneously fully God and fully human.

- Christians believe that through the sinless life, the crucifixion, and the resurrection of Jesus Christ, forgiveness of sins and the eternal life of God is offered to all those who believe, confessing Christ as their Lord.

"And that's it?" you might ask. "You are doing a disservice to these questioning students. What about all the other essential teachings you are completely overlooking?"

Here we arrive once more at this book's purpose. I've argued in this chapter, and throughout this section, that these *are* the essential teachings of the Christian faith. In the creeds we find summarized the fundamentals of what it takes to be a Scripture-oriented, Bible-believing Christian: belief in God the Father, God the Son, God the Holy Spirit, the Incarnation, Crucifixion, Resurrection, and Ascension of Christ, the universal Church, the final Resurrection of the dead, the final Judgment, and Eternity. There are certainly hundreds, or thousands, of other teachings within Christianity—but these listed beliefs are the ones that are primary.

In Part 2 of this book, we will now begin to look at the *non*-essentials; in other words, we'll discuss "What Believers Don't Have to Believe" even while maintaining their orthodox, Bible-believing status. I hope to bring up much of what unnecessarily divides Christ's Church today. We may disagree here or there on certain specific doctrines, but the fact that you have read this far in the book at the very least indicates your willingness to engage the question.

Shall we begin?

Questions for Reflection:

1. After reading this chapter, are you more or less inclined to accept the creeds as authoritative? Why or why not?

2. Is there anything in the creeds you find you do not personally believe? Which part(s)? Why?

3. Do you have any beliefs you think should have been included in the creeds? In other words, do you have any beliefs fundamental enough that they should be accepted by *all* Christians, but which are not specifically mentioned in any of the creedal statements we've examined? What are these beliefs?

4. If your answer to Question 3 is "Yes," and you find this fundamental belief you hold in my upcoming lists of "non-essential" and "unnecessarily divisive" beliefs, will you stop reading this book? Why or why not?

References

1) F.L. Cross and E.A. Livingstone, editors, *The Oxford Dictionary of the Christian Church.* 2nd edition. Oxford: Oxford University Press, 1989: 358.

2) C.S. Lewis, *Mere Christianity.* 1st paperback edition. New York: Macmillan, 1960: 119-120.

3) The Apostle's Creed:
  I believe in God the Father almighty, maker of heaven and earth; and in Jesus Christ his only Son, our Lord; who was conceived by the Holy Spirit, born of the Virgin Mary; suffered under Pontius Pilate, was crucified, dead, and buried; He descended into hell; the third day He rose again from the dead; He ascended into heaven, and sitteth on the right hand of God the Father almighty; from thence He shall come to judge the living and the dead. I believe in the Holy Spirit; the holy catholic church; the communion of saints; the forgiveness of sins; the resurrection of the body; and the life everlasting. Amen.

  The Nicene Creed:
  I believe in one God the Father Almighty; Maker of heaven and earth, and of all things visible and invisible. And in one Lord Jesus Christ, the only-begotten Son of God, begotten of the Father before all worlds, God of God, Light of Light, very God of very God, begotten, not made, being of one substance with the Father; by whom all things were made; who, for us men and for our salvation, came down from heaven, and was incarnate by the Holy Spirit of the Virgin Mary, and was made man; and was crucified also for us under Pontius Pilate; He suffered and was buried; and the third day He rose again, according to the Scriptures; and ascended into heaven, and sitteth on the right hand of the Father; and He shall come again, with glory, to judge both the living and the dead; whose kingdom shall have no end. And I believe in the Holy Spirit, the Lord and Giver of life; who proceedeth from the Father and the Son; who with the Father and the Son together is worshipped and glorified; who spoke by the prophets. And I believe in one

holy catholic and apostolic church. I acknowledge one baptism for the remission of sins; and I look for the resurrection of the dead, and the life of the world to come. Amen.

The Athanasian Creed:
We worship one God in trinity, and trinity in unity, neither confounding the Persons nor dividing the substance. For the Person of the Father is one; of the Son, another; of the Holy Spirit, another. But the divinity of the Father and of the Son and of the Holy Spirit is one, the glory equal, the majesty equal. Such as is the Father, such also is the Son, and such the Holy Spirit. The Father is uncreated, the Son is uncreated, the Holy Spirit is uncreated. The Father is infinite, the Son is infinite, the Holy Spirit is infinite. The Father is eternal, the Son is eternal, the Holy Spirit is eternal. And yet there are not three eternal Beings, but one eternal Being. So also there are not three uncreated Beings, nor three infinite Beings, but one uncreated and one infinite Being. In like manner, the Father is omnipotent, the Son is omnipotent, and the Holy Spirit is omnipotent. And yet there are not three omnipotent Beings, but one omnipotent Being. Thus the Father is God, the Son is God, and the Holy Spirit is God. And yet there are not three Gods, but one God only. The Father is Lord, the Son is Lord, and the Holy Spirit is Lord. And yet there are not three Lords, but one Lord only. For as we are compelled by Christian truth to confess each person distinctively to be both God and Lord, we are prohibited by the Catholic religion to say that there are three Gods or Lords. The Father is made by none, nor created, nor begotten. The Son is from the Father alone, not made, not created, but begotten. The Holy Spirit is not created by the Father and the Son, nor begotten, but proceeds. Therefore, there is one Father, not three Fathers; one Son, not three Sons; one Holy Spirit, not three Holy Spirits. And in this Trinity there is nothing prior or posterior, nothing greater or less, but all three persons are coeternal and coequal to themselves. So that through all, as was said above, both unity in trinity and trinity in unity is to be adored. Whoever would be saved, let him think thus concerning the Trinity.

4) Stuart Briscoe, *The Apostles' Creed: Beliefs that Matter.* Wheaton, Illinois: Harold Shaw Publishers, 1994: 3.

5) Cyril C. Richardson, editor, *Early Christian Fathers.* 4th printing. New York: Macmillan, 1978: 22.

6) G. W. Bromley, "Creed, Creeds." *Evangelical Dictionary of Theology.* Edited by Walter A. Elwell. Grand Rapids, Michigan: Baker Books, 1984: 283-84.

7) Tertullian, *The Prescription Against Heretics.* Trans. by Peter Holmes. *Ante-Nicene Fathers, Volume Three. Latin Christianity: Its Founder, Tertullian.* Edited by Alexander Roberts and James Donaldson. Revised by A. Cleveland Coxe. 2nd printing. Peabody, Mass.: Hendrickson Publishers, 1999: 249.

8) 1 Cor. 8:6.

9) 1 Cor. 15:3-7.

10) 1 Timothy 3:16.

11) John Henry Cardinal Newman, *An Essay on the Development of Christian Doctrine.* 1878 edition. Chapter 4, Section 3: 148-49. newmanreader.org.

12) Vincent of Lérins, *A Commonitory*. Trans. by C.A. Heurtley. *Nicene and Post-Nicene Fathers, Volume Eleven*. Edited by Philip Schaff and Henry Wace. 2nd series. 4th printing. Peabody, Mass.: Hendrickson Publishers, 2004: 147-48.

13) Steve Ray, *Upon This Rock*. San Francisco: Ignatius Press, 1999: 184.

14) John Henry Cardinal Newman, *An Essay on the Development of Christian Doctrine*. 1878 edtion. Introduction, Section 19: 27. newmanreader.org.

15) Taken from the BBC videocassette series *The Long Search*. *Orthodox Christianity: The Rumanian Solution*. New York: Ambrose Video, 1978.

16) In his *Essay*, Introduction, Sections 7-10.

17) Norman L. Geisler and Ralph E. MacKenzie, *Roman Catholics and Evangelicals: Agreements and Differences*. 8th printing. Grand Rapids, Michigan: Baker Books, 2002: 459.

18) Exodus 3:14; Hebrews 11:6.

19) Genesis 1:1; Hebrews 1:1-2.

20) John 1:1, 14; John 10:36; Matthew 1:23; 1 Timothy 3:16.

21) Mark 15:15; John 19:33; Acts 2:31; Acts 1:9.

22) Matthew 25:31-46; 2 Timothy 4:1.

23) Matthew 28:19; John 14:26; 2 Cor. 13:14; 1 John 5:7.

24) 1 Cor. 12:12-13, 20; Ephesians 1:7; 4:4-6, 15-16.

25) John 6:39-40; Phil. 1:23; Rev. 21:4; Daniel 12:2-3.

Part 2: Five Specific Issues

Chapter 3: Six Days

"If we don't agree that the Bible teaches six literal days . . . and we don't read the text as written, right there in Genesis 1, we've lost the battle. . . . If you're an individual, a church, or a denomination, and you say that we don't have to agree on the literal six days of creation, you've lost the battle."—from a Christian minister.

"[F]ar too many of us still make the intellectually suicidal mistake of thinking that promoting 'creation science' is the best way to resist naturalistic philosophies of science."—from a Christian historian.

Is God a Creationist?—book title.

The Supernatural Creation

Both the Bible and the creeds open with the same statement: The universe we inhabit was created by God. "In the beginning God created the heaven and the earth."[1] Because of this, Christians do not think of the universe as meaningless or without purpose; rather, the universal creation evidences purpose, meaning, and providential care. It appears designed by an Intelligence in some respects incomprehensible, but in some respects analogous to our own. This is what the Bible tells us we should expect, given that "God created man in His own image; in the image of God created He him; male and female created He them."[2] Although God as Creator possesses a qualitatively different level of existence than our existence as created beings, He is not entirely beyond our ken, since He has granted us also to be creative beings within our own scope. By way of analogy with our knowledge of ourselves, we can know something of God the Creator, transcendent from and yet immanent within his creation, even as artists are separate from their artwork and yet stand revealed within it. Our own creativity and designing intelligence are faint echoes of the great Designer of existence.

So the "Who?" of creation is answered: "We believe in God the Father Almighty, creator of heaven and earth." The "Why?" of creation also has a biblical answer: All things exist because of the immense love and care with which God has condescended to bless his creatures. He did not, after all, *have* to create us, but love compelled Him. In the Christian understanding, the fact of existence itself demonstrates God's love. All Christians are in basic agreement on these statements. Out of his love, God created the universe, which thus manifests the purpose and design of its Maker: "The heavens declare the glory of God; and the firmament sheweth His handiwork."[3]

On the other hand, when we arrive at the "How?" of creation, we begin to find disagreement. As John Wilson, editor of the Christian magazine *Books and Culture*, puts it, "As Christians we all acknowledge that God made us. But we may differ—we *will* differ—in our understanding of how that making unfolded." He continues:

> Many Christians are raised to believe that they are faced with a stark choice: Either they accept the most literal Young Earth account of Creation or they abandon their faith.[4]

However, this either / or choice may not be the entire story. Many more seemingly valid interpretations of the biblical story of creation are available to us, some of which I'll discuss later in this chapter.

Proponents of Young Earth creationism—the view that the six days of creation recorded in Genesis 1 are six literal 24-hour days, and that the universe, the earth, and / or the human race are about 6,000 years old—often are quite explicit in their commitment to this "stark choice" Wilson mentions. For example, Ken Ham, a well known Young Earth creationist, argues in his book *Why Won't They Listen?* that acceptance of this interpretation of creation is a prerequisite for effective Christian witness and evangelism:

> Have you ever noticed that when the topic of evolution, or millions of years, comes up, there's an incredible emotional reaction? Why? Because that's where the enemy has gained ground; this is where the battle is at.
>
> After all these years, I'm still amazed that the Christian community largely misses the direction of the battle for the hearts and minds of men, women, and children.
>
> As I've stated, ministries like *Answers in Genesis* [Rev. Ham's own ministry] are frequently accused of being divisive. I must press the point, however, that the foundational parts of the Bible are the real key.
>
> If we don't agree that the Bible teaches six literal days . . . and we don't read the text as written, right there in Genesis 1, we've lost the battle. . . . If you're an individual, a church, or a denomination, and you say that we don't have to agree on the literal six days of creation, you've lost the battle.[5]

Henry M. Morris, even better known than Ham for his many years of Young-Earth apologetics, makes a similar point for the primary importance of accepting Young-Earth dating for the sake of biblical interpretation and evangelism:

> The idea that the earth is billions of years old and the forms of life on the earth have been gradually changing and increasing in complexity during those vast ages seems to be *prima facie* evidence of evolution and against

the Bible. The almost universal indoctrination in this geologic-age concept is beyond question *the major barrier against acceptance of the divine inspiration of the Bible and the truth of Christianity* [emphasis added].[6]

For these writers and others like them, the truths of God's existence and Christ's redemptive mission, along with other biblical teachings, will assuredly be cast aside by non-Christians once the belief in a literal six-day creation is abandoned. This loss of faith will occur, in their view (and already has occurred to a large extent), because any suggestion that the creation story of Genesis 1 might not be a *literally* exact account will inevitably lead to disbelief or at least incredulity toward the rest of the Bible, including the Gospel stories of Christ's life, death, and resurrection. Non-believers' rejection of the literalness of Genesis 1 is the answer to the question, as Ken Ham's book title has it, *Why Won't They* [non-Christians] *Listen?*

On the other hand, it does not seem to have occurred to these authors that perhaps the exact opposite may be a cause of widespread loss of faith. Perhaps some people have become disbelieving or incredulous of biblical truth as the result of Christians insisting on interpretations of Genesis (specifically, the interpretations known collectively as "creation science") which seem patently at odds with the history of scientific discoveries. Further, as a teacher, I've seen far too many Christians who seem to develop "split personalities" when it comes to reconciling what they're taught by well-meaning fellow Christians with what seems scientifically obvious, but is contrary to Young-Earth doctrines. I've even had students tell me, "I believe one thing at church and something else in the classroom"—as if God had decided to author confusion after all.[7] Because of this vacillation, not only do these Christians miss the benefit of the rigorous scientific analysis of creation, but they also miss out on the primary point of the creation story, that of God's magnificence:

> [T]he extended descriptions of creation in the first chapters of Genesis . . . are not to be viewed as providing a scientific account of the origin of the universe. They are religious statements, designed to show God's glory and greatness.[8]

In other words, it is not the case that the Bible necessarily clashes with scientific discovery, but it perhaps *is* the case that scientific discovery clashes with some Christians' *interpretations* of the Bible. And, as Augustine put it 1600 years ago, when historical or scientific discoveries are found to be in conflict with our biblical interpretations, we should take a hard look first of all, not at the discoveries, but at our interpretations. In his article "Augustine and the Interpretation of Genesis," writer Phil Dowe paraphrases Augustine's position:

> There may also be external reasons for not accepting the literal interpretation of Scripture. This is where science enters the picture. These external reasons also rely on the premise that there is one God who has produced both creation and Scripture. This means that it is impossible that

we should find science contradicting Scripture, or Scripture contradicting science. Augustine's sense of "science" refers to that science which is conclusively proven and contradicts Scripture. In such cases, Scripture must be taken metaphorically. In fact, it is only in cases where science has been conclusively proven, that we may reinterpret Scripture.

Augustine also urges that Christians must not be what he calls "doggedly literal minded" in continuing to insist on a literal interpretation of Scripture in the face of proven science. He warns that Christians who do not take this advice will bring shame to their religion and its Scripture and prevent people from ever coming to accept what is important in Scripture.[9]

This seems important enough to repeat: "Christians who do not take this advice will bring shame to their religion and its Scripture and prevent people from ever coming to accept what is important in Scripture." Could this be another answer to Ken Ham's question *Why Won't They Listen?*

Contrary to some Young-Earth creationists,[10] taking Augustine's advice regarding the interpretation of Scripture does not mean we must place the authority of scientific findings over the authority of the Bible, as if God's Word were "outranked" by advances in scientific knowledge. However, it is true that Augustine would place the authority of scientific knowledge over tendentious and arguable *interpretations* of the Bible. Is it possible that if only the past century or so of literalist Christians had heeded Augustine's advice, much of the ballyhooed "science versus religion" debate could have been avoided outright?

If the reader thinks I'm being overly critical of "creation science" advocates, other Christians are far sterner. "[F]ar too many of us still make the intellectually suicidal mistake of thinking that promoting 'creation science' is the best way to resist naturalistic philosophies of science," argues Mark Noll, professor of history at Wheaton College and author of several books on Christian intellectual history, notably *The Scandal of the Evangelical Mind*.[11] The "naturalism" to which Noll refers is the anti-biblical philosophical presupposition "that everything is natural, i.e., that everything there is belongs to the world of nature, and so can be studied by the methods appropriate for studying that world, and the apparent exceptions can be somehow explained away."[12] Even when found in scientists, naturalism is a philosophical stance, of course, not a result of scientific findings; this remains true even though science proceeds via "methodological" naturalism, i.e., the assumption that physical processes and events have a naturalistic cause.

Therefore, naturalism can be resisted philosophically without recourse to "creation science." Under the guise of science, writers such as Richard Dawkins and Carl Sagan put forth naturalistic atheism as though it were the scientific "default position," which it is not. Philosophical naturalism (as opposed to "methodological" naturalism) is a *philosophy*. These writers' anti-religious presuppositions should be exposed wherever they are discovered, as they under the mantle of scientific authority try illegitimately to smuggle in a philosophical worldview which cannot be proven scientifically.

But then why is the promotion of creation science "intellectually suicidal," as Noll puts it? If naturalistic philosophies should be resisted, why not enlist allies in the creation-science camp? By way of reply, I'd like you to enter into a thought experiment with me. On his ministry's website, Ken Ham relates a somewhat similar thought experiment:

> Recently, one of our associates sat down with a highly respected world-class Hebrew scholar and asked him this question: "If you started with the Bible alone, without considering any outside influences whatsoever, could you ever come up with millions or billions of years of history for the Earth and universe?" The answer from this scholar? "Absolutely not!"[13]

However, I'd like to go a step further with this. Let's also ask the follow-up question, "If not for a certain reading of 'the Bible alone,' as Ken Ham puts it, would we come up with an age of 6,000 years for the earth and the universe?" Here follows our imaginative experiment:

No Darwin: Imagine that Darwin's *Origin of Species* was never published, and no other similar work has appeared in the time either before or since 1859. So there is no "Darwinian evolutionary theory" to conflict with our interpretations of revealed Scripture, no history of court battles or public debates, no knowledge of this theory at all on the part of anyone, including all scientists and all the general public.

No Genesis: Now imagine further (this may be more of a stretch): There is no Genesis 1-3. There is no account of creation in the Bible *at all*, and never has been. Jews and Christians have no revealed, scriptural creation story, and thus no interpretations of that story, whether "literal" or not. There is no indication in the Bible or elsewhere as to the age of the universe or the speed with which it appeared. All we have for knowledge of our origins is what we can discover with absolutely no *a priori* intellectual, philosophical, or religious commitments of any kind whatsoever.

Do you have this experiment firmly in your mind? Now answer these questions, please (and remember—no appeals either to Genesis or to Darwin):

- Based on their investigations of the galaxies, would astronomers arrive at a figure of 6,000 years for the age of the universe?
- Based on their investigations of its strata, would geologists arrive at a figure of 6,000 years for the age of the earth?
- Based on their investigations of the variety of living organisms, would biologists arrive at a figure of 6,000 years for the age of the existence of life on earth?
- Based on their investigations of fossil remains and artifacts, would paleontologists, archeologists, and anthropologists arrive at a figure of 6,000 years for the age of the human race?

I am assuming you are being honest with yourself. Therefore, I am further assuming that your answer is to all of these questions, "No, of course not. On all of these counts, the evidence obviously points to a much greater age." Here we arrive at the point of this thought experiment: The 6,000-year figure for the age of the universe, earth, or human race, obviously could not have arisen scientifically or by an unbiased examination of the evidence. It arose from a certain reading of the Book of Genesis, or from those who examine natural evidence with an eye toward "scientifically proving" their reading of Genesis. Thus the primary activities of Young-Earth creation scientists seem to me to be (1) trying to come up with evidence for a presupposition which is inherently implausible to begin with; and (2) trying to explain away all contrary evidence, no matter in what field it may appear.

An argument might come to your mind, however: "Well, all right, but that's precisely why we *need* the creation account of the Bible: so our investigations could be directed by our revealed, *a priori* knowledge of the Earth's young age. Otherwise, if not for this revelation in Genesis, we might not know of our limited history, and we would fall into the numerous time-frame mistakes you are bringing up. This could be a way God is testing our faith, to see whether we'll believe our own scientific investigations or believe His Word." (By the way, I'm not inventing this argument; I've heard it made.)

However, keep in mind that if you accept this argument, you must also accept the conception of God as being almost completely deceptive, and the conception of God's creation as being almost completely misleading. Given the Young-Earth view, almost every field of scientific inquiry involving the age of the universe, the earth, or life on earth, must inevitably arrive at wrong conclusions, because God has already "stacked the deck" against all such investigations. As a theistic Christian who worships an absolutely perfect God Who is all Truth and Who cannot lie,[14] I cannot accept the argument for revealed truth based on the need to explain a deceptive Creator and a deceptive creation. The universe is supposed to *reveal* the glory of God, not conceal it.

Young-Earth creationism, in other words, seems—if I may say so—rather disrespectful of God's character. It has to explain why all of God's handiwork actually means something completely different from what it appears to mean, and also why God decided to create all things with this misleading appearance.

And please note well: It is only this single interpretation of the Bible which causes all this difficulty. If you don't begin with the presupposition of the literal six-day creation happening 6,000 years ago, you don't even *need* to argue against the scientific discoveries taking place in all the different fields of study I mentioned. "Nowhere is the problem of interpretation more pronounced than in understanding the biblical idea of creation," two evangelical authors assert. "[T]he *timing* of creation has tended to cloud the real issue of the *fact* of creation [emphasis added]."[15] It seems that some Christians have elevated the statement "The universe is 6,000 years old" to the same level of importance as the biblical and creedal statement "The universe was created by God." However, this elevation is neither right nor necessary. As one work states:

The changes in the traditional picture of creation brought about by increased scientific knowledge (astronomical, geological, paleontological, biological) since the beginning of the nineteenth century have at times caused much religious unsettlement to orthodox Christians. But though they must radically affect our view of the order, dating, and character of the events (and hence also the degree to which the Old Testament can be conceived as a scientific book), *they hardly touch the fundamental philosophical questions which surround the notion of creation. These remain in essentials unaffected* [emphasis added].[16]

It is essential that Christians believe in God's design and creation of all really existing things, including our universe and ourselves. However, because of the existence of several varied biblical interpretations of creation, each convincing in its own right, belief in a literal six-day creation of the universe is not an essential component of the Christian faith. In fact, creation science's many monumental efforts to prove a literal six-day creation occurring a few thousand years ago seem to be a well intentioned but misdirected waste of time and energy, and may even end up causing more harm to Christians than help. *The literal six-day creation is not a crucial belief* for all Christians to hold.

Earlier, I quoted Mark Noll's reference to the "naturalistic philosophies of science." Here, in my judgment, lies the *real* "science versus religion" controversy: not "What are the specific mechanisms and time-frames of the universe's origins?" but rather, "Is naturalism true or is supernaturalism true? Does the universe as we have it today require a Designer existing outside of and independently of the universe, or is it a more or less happenstance concatenation of purely material events?" I'd like to turn now to this question, the question of evidences for intelligent design in creation.

Questions for Reflection:

1. Do you think of people who believe the universe is billions of years old as being anti-biblical? Do you think of them as being misguided?

2. Do you think of people who believe the universe is approximately 6,000 years old as being unintelligent? Do you think of them as being misguided?

3. Have you ever heard interpretations of Genesis 1 besides the literal one? What are they? What do you think of them?

4. If you had heard the author making the argument of this chapter in a college classroom, would you think the author was non-Christian? Would you think the author was attacking Christian faith? Attacking the Bible?

Six Days

Intelligence and Design

In June of 2000, I first heard Michael Shermer speak. Shermer, editor of *Skeptic Magazine* and self-avowed atheist, was a key figure in a conference entitled "Design and Its Critics," put on by Concordia University, a Christian college. The conference explored the "Intelligent Design" concept—the idea that evidence for the purposeful, intelligent design of natural phenomena exists, given the age of the universe and the mathematical / biological improbabilities of certain entities, functions, and processes arising in nature by chance. Further, the concept of Intelligent Design directly implies the need for a purposeful, intelligent Designer of nature, Who must also exist outside of or transcending nature. Needless to say, as an evangelistic atheist, Shermer was part of the "Critics" side of the presentations.

At one point in his keynote address, Shermer ran through several overhead projections of the creation stories and deities of various cultures. He argued that "the belief that the findings of science just happen to coincide with one particular religious faith to the exclusion of the thousands of others in the world is both exclusionary and untenable."[17] Therefore, according to Shermer, Intelligent Design arguments were just a re-packaged way of getting Christian creationist claims into schools by giving them flashier scientific credentials. His idea seemed to be that the multiplicity of creation stories proved that we could not privilege the Genesis account, even if the Judeo-Christian story were decked out in Designer clothing.

However, I remember having a different reaction. "Have I missed his point entirely?" I thought to myself. "Surely all he's proven is that virtually every culture throughout history has believed that the universe was intelligently designed! This is *not* solely a Judeo-Christian belief." The rest of Shermer's presentations throughout the conference did nothing to dissuade my conviction of his argumentative stumble.

In other words, as biochemist Michael Behe (also a presenter at the same conference[18]) points out, "The conclusion of intelligent design flows naturally from the data itself—not from sacred books or sectarian beliefs." The failure of people such as Michael Shermer to reach this conclusion is not due to lack of evidence, according to Behe, but rather due to a philosophical mindset which presupposes that Intelligent Design cannot be a viable scientific conclusion. This mindset causes some to overlook or undervalue evidence they would neither overlook nor undervalue were it not for their philosophical presuppositions:

> Imagine a room in which a body lies crushed, flat as a pancake. A dozen detectives crawl around, examining the floor with magnifying glasses for any clue to the identity of the perpetrator. In the middle of the room, next to the body, stands a large, gray elephant. The detectives carefully avoid bumping into the pachyderm's legs as they crawl, and never even glance at it. Over time the detectives get frustrated with their lack of progress but resolutely press on, looking even more closely at the floor. You see,

textbooks say detectives must "get their man," so they never consider elephants.

There is an elephant in the roomful of scientists who are trying to explain the development of life. The elephant is labeled "intelligent design." To a person who does not feel obliged to restrict his search to unintelligent causes, the straightforward conclusion is that many biochemical systems were designed. They were designed not by the laws of nature, not by chance and necessity; rather, they were *planned*.[19]

This primary philosophical presupposition of science, this obligation to find only "unintelligent causes," is called "methodological naturalism"—that is, the methods of science rely on the naturalistic mindset, and rule out of bounds from the start any non-naturalistic explanation of phenomena (such as "The thunder was caused by Zeus" or "I prayed and God healed me"). This method, of course, has been highly productive in discovering natural mechanisms behind events (the "How" of nature), but must inevitably lead to a dead end should evidence begin pointing toward a "Who," as in a Designer of these natural mechanisms.

The current impasse in origin-of-life scenarios has been frankly confessed by some, such as biochemist Klaus Dose:

> More than thirty years of experimentation on the origin of life in the fields
> of chemical and molecular evolution have led to a better perception of the
> immensity of the problem of the origin of life on Earth rather than to its
> solution. At present all discussions . . . either end in stalemate or in a
> confession of ignorance.[20]

Could this stalemate be the result of the method of investigation itself? As particle physicist Walter Bradley says, "If [naturalistic scientists] are persuaded ahead of time that there isn't a God, then no matter how compelling the evidence, they'll always say, 'Wait and we'll find something better in the future.' But that's a metaphysical argument. . . . [W]hat I've found is absolutely overwhelming evidence that points toward an Intelligent Designer."[21]

"Absolutely overwhelming evidence" is a strong phrase. The fields of biochemistry, information science, and so on, could provide us some examples of that evidence. However, to find an exemplar of this type of "overwhelming" evidence, I'd like to focus on another branch of science, that of astronomical physics, and discuss what has been called the "Anthropic Principle."

Paraphrased, the Anthropic Principle runs something like this: "If we as intelligent beings are able to observe the features of the universe, at least we know one sure feature of the universe from the outset: It has to be a universe capable of sustaining intelligent beings like us." This might sound simplistic, or even simple-minded, but it does contain a powerful truth, as we'll see.

Questions for Reflection:

1. If science is given enough time, do you think it will eventually discover a non-supernatural cause of life and all existence? Why or why not? If there is a supernatural cause of life and all existence, will science be able to find *that*? Why or why not?

2. Do you find Michael Shermer's argument, as filtered through me, persuasive? Did he have a valid point and I missed it?

3. Michael Behe says, "The conclusion of intelligent design flows naturally from the data itself." Do you think this is true? Or is the concept of intelligent design only convincing to those who already believe in God?

4. Is the concept of a non-designed universe arising by chance only convincing to those who already *don't* believe in God?

The Anthropic Principle

The anthropic principle is not a new idea in scientific literature. In 1955, G.J. Whithrow argued in a British scientific journal that a "variety of astronomical conditions must be met if the universe is to be habitable."[22] This is certainly a central premise of the anthropic principle, although the term "anthropic principle" itself was first used by astronomer Brandon Carter in a 1974 publication of the International Astronomical Union and later elaborated by him in more extensive works. The astronomical conditions that must be met for the rise of intelligent life are so extensive in reach and varied in instance, they are often referred to as "anthropic coincidences"—in other words, coincidences necessary for the existence of *anthropos*, man.

"An anthropic coincidence," according to University of Texas philosophy professor Robert C. Koons, "consists of some feature of the laws of nature, the fundamental constituents of matter, or the initial condition of the universe, that had to take a value within some interval in order for life (and hence, for human observers) to exist at all." The "coincidental" description of these features of the universe arises because of the extraordinarily narrow intervals of value necessary for them to produce life: "Consequently, the universe is in some sense 'fine-tuned' for the possibility of complex chemistry and thus of life." He goes on to categorize these coincidences into four types:

- Features of the fundamental laws of nature, including the relative strengths of fundamental forces and other physical constants.

- Characteristics of the fundamental particles of matter.

- The size, degree of flatness and smoothness, and rate of expansion of matter emerging from the Big Bang.

- Features of the solar system and the earth (this is the only type of coincidences not universally characteristic, but locally necessary for life on earth itself).[23]

"So what?" the skeptic might object. "All this proves is that we were cosmically lucky. And most of these 'coincidences' will prove to have naturalistic explanations, anyway. You make too quick a jump from 'The universe appears to have some extremely fortunate (for us) features,' to 'There must be a Designer.' Given enough time, who knows what might have happened?"

On the surface, this seems to be a valid objection. "[I]t is more than likely," according to theoretical particle physicist Stephen M. Barr, "that at least some of the facts about the laws of physics that appear favorable to our existence do have conventional scientific explanations." However, Barr immediately goes on to say:

> Even if that proved true of all of them, however, it would not explain away the coincidental nature of these facts. The critical point was well expressed by the noted astrophysicists Bernard Carr and Martin Rees: "One day we may have a more physical explanation for some of the relationships . . . that now seem genuine coincidences. . . . However, even if all apparently anthropic coincidences could be explained in this way, it would still be remarkable that the relationships dictated by physical theory happened also to be those propitious for life."[24]

So then, what are these "remarkable" relationships, these "anthropic coincidences" which are pointing many toward a specific belief in design, both at the universal and the planetary level?

In an article entitled "Design and the Anthropic Principle," astronomer Hugh Ross highlights several of these coincidences, so many, in fact, that a bare review of just of few of them will have to suffice (the following list consists of edited excerpts from Ross's article). The first few cover what Robert Koons calls "features of the fundamental laws of nature, including the relative strengths of fundamental forces and other physical constants":

- The gravitational coupling constant (i.e., the force of gravity) determines what kinds of stars are possible in the universe. If the force were even slightly stronger, stars would be larger, but would burn too unevenly and rapidly to support life; if the force were even slightly weaker, stars would be smaller than our own sun and thus unable to produce the heavy elements necessary for planetary life.

- The strong nuclear force coupling constant holds together the particles in the nucleus of an atom. If it were slightly weaker, multi-proton nuclei would not hold together, and hydrogen would be the only element in the universe. If this force were slightly stronger, the supply of both hydrogen and the various life-essential elements heavier than iron would be insufficient for the possibility of life.

- The weak nuclear force coupling constant affects the behavior of leptons, a class of elementary particles that do not participate in strong nuclear reactions (the behavior of this force is seen most commonly in radioactivity). After the Big Bang, the availability of neutrons (a type of lepton) determined the amount of helium produced. If the weak nuclear force coupling constant were slightly larger, neutrons would be less available, and therefore would produce little or no helium. Without this helium, heavy elements sufficient for the constructing of life would not be made by the internal reactions of stars. If the weak nuclear force coupling constant were slightly smaller, most or all hydrogen would have been converted into helium, and thus too *many* heavy elements would have been made for life to exist.

- The electromagnetic coupling constant binds electrons to protons in atoms. If the electromagnetic coupling constant were slightly smaller, no electrons would be held in orbits about nuclei. If it were slightly larger, an atom could not "share" an electron orbit with other atoms. Either way, molecules, and hence life, would be impossible.

Ross also discusses what Koons calls "characteristics of the fundamental particles of matter":

- The ratio of electron to proton mass determines the characteristics of the orbits of electrons about nuclei. If the electron to proton mass ratio were slightly larger or slightly smaller, again, molecules would not form, and life would be impossible.

- If the rate of proton decay were any faster, the level of radiation in the universe would be lethal. If the rate were any slower, the universe would not have enough matter in it to make life possible.

Next Ross turns to "the size, degree of flatness and smoothness, and rate of expansion of matter emerging from the Big Bang":

- The age of the universe governs what kinds of stars exist. If the universe were just a couple of billion years younger, no environment suitable for life would exist. [My own comment on this: Often we hear atheists talking about the incomprehensible size and age of the universe as showing us that a personal God could not possibly be interested in us, we tiny specks in the cosmos. However, this particular anthropic coincidence seems to indicate that, given the speed of light, the universe *has* to be at least as old and large as it is to support intelligent life. In other words, the size and age of the universe again point toward human life.]

- The expansion rate of the universe determines what kinds of stars, if any, form in the universe. If the rate of expansion were slightly less, the whole universe would have recollapsed before any solar-type stars could have settled into a stable burning phase. If the universe were expanding slightly more rapidly, no galaxies (and hence no stars) would condense from the general expansion.

- The rate at which entropy seems to be occurring in the universe affects the condensation of massive systems. If the entropy rate for the universe were slightly larger, no galactic systems would form (and therefore no stars). If the entropy level were slightly smaller, the galactic systems that formed would effectively trap radiation and prevent any fragmentation of the systems into stars. Either way the universe would be devoid of stars and thus of life.

- The mass of the universe determines how much nuclear burning takes place as the universe cools after the Big Bang. If the mass were slightly larger, stars could not sustain life; if slightly smaller, planets like ours could not form.

- The universe is just flat and smooth enough to develop stars and galaxies. However, if it were any flatter and smoother, these may not have developed, at least not in a way capable of sustaining life.

- The relationships among the atomic nuclei of various elements are precisely such that an abundance of elements essential to life can be manufactured (Ross's article provides a great deal more detail, for those versed in biochemistry).

- The average distance between stars in our part of the galaxy is about 30 trillion miles. If this distance were slightly smaller, the resulting combined gravitational force would be so strong as to destabilize planetary orbits. If this distance were slightly larger, the debris thrown out by supernovae would be so thinly distributed that rocky planets like earth would never form. The average distance between stars is just right to make possible a planetary system such as our own.

- After the hydrogen fusion process begins in a sun, luminosity increase also begins. If the rate of increase is too large, a greenhouse effect would eliminate any possible life on surrounding planets. If the rate is too small, liquid water could not exist, again eliminating the possibility of life.

The next type of anthropic coincidences, according to Koons, involves "features of the solar system and the earth." As Ross notes, "It is not just the universe that bears evidence for design. The earth itself reveals such evidence." He lists nineteen features of the sun / earth relationship conducive to life, including the following:

- Parent star age.
- Parent star distance from center of galaxy.
- Parent star mass.
- Parent star color.
- Surface gravity of planet.
- Distance from parent star.
- Thickness of crust.
- Rotation period.
- Oxygen to nitrogen ratio in atmosphere.
- Carbon dioxide and water vapor levels in atmosphere.
- Atmospheric electric discharge rate.

It is little wonder Ross concludes, "It seems abundantly clear that the earth, too, in addition to the universe, has experienced divine design."[25]

The probabilities we are discussing are too large to comprehend. Take just one of the above universal constants: the expansion rate of the universe. According to astronomer Alan Guth, this expansion rate, in order to produce the stars and galaxies we inhabit, had to fall within a value of one chance out of 10 to the 55th power.[26] And that's just one "coincidence"! Here's another, taken from astrophysicist and atheist Steven Weinberg: If the energy of the Big Bang were different by one part out of 10 to the 120th power, there would be no life anywhere in our universe.[27]

When all of these features are taken together, the odds against life of any type, let alone intelligent life, are beyond astronomical. It's as if a lottery with prizes of a new house and a guaranteed lifetime income were held between one human and a quadrillion rocks, each numbered separately and given its own lottery ticket—and the lone human just happened to win. It wouldn't be too much of a stretch to suspect the whole thing was rigged by Someone behind the scenes.

However, does all this really add up to a Creator?

Since the death of Bertrand Russell, probably the most famous philosophical atheist in the world during most of my life has been Antony Flew. His 1950 article "Theology and Falsification" is required reading for any philosophy or religion major in college; more recently he has published "The Presumption of Atheism" and many other articles and books, including a book-length debate over the existence of God with Christian theist William Lane Craig.

While I was working on this chapter, an Associated Press article was released (Dec. 9, 2004): "Famous Atheist Now Believes in God." Here are some excerpts:

> At age 81, after decades of insisting belief is a mistake, Antony Flew has concluded that some sort of intelligence or first cause must have created the universe. A super-intelligence is the only good explanation for the origin of life and the complexity of nature, Flew said. . . . [He does not believe in the personal God Christians believe in, but] "It could be a person in the sense of a being that has intelligence and a purpose. . . ."
>
> [I]f his belief upsets people, "Well, that's too bad," Flew said. "My whole life has been guided by the principle of Plato's Socrates: Follow the evidence, wherever it leads."[28]

According to another writer, Flew's intellectual reversal "is the product not of a personal conversion, but of reasoned analysis of the latest scientific data."[29]

Does the evidence for the intelligent design of the universe add up? If we follow the evidence wherever it leads, does it lead to a Designer? It seems at least reasonable to conclude that it does.

Questions for Reflection:

1. Whenever astronomical and mathematical calculations are discussed, many people's eyes tend to glaze over. What about you? Did you find these "anthropic coincidences" convincing? Why or why not?

2. Do you think of these evidences of design as convincing only to those who are already convinced? Why or why not? What about the case of Antony Flew?

3. A biologist friend of mine argues that, since most of these examples come from particle physicists, astronomers, chemists, mathematicians, information scientists, and so on, they are not completely convincing to those who study actual

living organisms themselves, i.e., biologists. What do you think of his argument? Does he have a point? Why or why not?

4. If life on earth actually was intelligently designed by God, should a biologist be able to detect that design? Why or why not? What about a biologist working within the presupposition of "methodological naturalism"?

5. What would you think about intelligent design if we find life elsewhere in the universe? Would this challenge your beliefs or support them?

Alternative Interpretations of Genesis 1

Even if you found compelling the evidence for the Intelligent Design of the universe, only a little of which I summarized above,[30] you probably noticed something in the discussion which may have been a bit disturbing. You probably noticed that almost all of the listed "anthropic coincidences" presuppose a very old universe. In other words, we've come back around to the question with which we began: Can one be a believing, biblically-oriented Christian and still reject the literal six-day account of Creation? Obviously, I think this is possible, but why? What valid alternatives are there to the literalistic interpretation?

Jonathan Sarfati, a staunch Young-Earth six-day creationist, reasonably assents in his book *Refuting Compromise* (a book, by the way, primarily directed against the teaching of Hugh Ross, discussed above) that one can reject six-day creationism and still be a Christian: "[O]ne does not need to believe in six-day creation to be saved. . . . We know that people can be genuine Christians . . . even if they don't accept creation in six 24-hour days."[31] However, I propose something quite a bit more than this reasonable assent—I propose that one can reject literal six-day creationism and not only be a Christian, but be a Scripture-oriented Christian who accepts the Bible as the infallible, inspired Word of God Himself. Further, one can accept a different interpretation of the Creation account than the literal and still find oneself in the company of many notable fellow Christians throughout the history of the Christian Church.

Let's explore three of these different understandings (obviously this list is not exhaustive). The alternative interpretations of Genesis 1 to be discussed are the following: (1) what I will call the *Literary* interpretation; (2) the *Allegorical* interpretation; (3) and the *Scientific Correspondence* interpretation.

(1) The Literary interpretation:

"And the earth was without form, and void; and darkness was upon the face of the deep. And the Spirit of God moved upon the face of the waters."[32] Here we see a kind of primal chaos out of which God's creative action brings order and life. However, notice that the act of creation resolves two different types of difficulties: The earth is "without form," so it needs to be "formed"; and the earth is "void" (empty), so its "form" also needs to be filled or populated with the appropriate beings.

Some have pointed out a literary device in the remainder of Genesis 1, in which the first three days of creating the necessary "forms" exactly parallel the second three days of creating the necessary "populations" of those forms. We might label this two-part structure the "realms of existence" and the "inhabitants of the realms" of existence. This structure would look something like this:

Realms of existence:	**Inhabitants of the realms:**
Day 1: Light is created.	Day 4: The stars, sun, and moon are created.
Day 2: The waters and sky are created.	Day 5: Water creatures and flying creatures are created.
Day 3: Dry land and vegetation are created.	Day 6: Land animals and humans are created.

The most immediately striking point to these parallels in the days of creation is that it does not seem that the "days" of creation refer to periods of time at all! Rather, the seven-day week merely serves as a handy literary device by which to structure the manifold splendors of creation (in six days) and God's pleasure in the wondrous accomplishment (on the seventh). This structure is later made the weekly model for time-encased humans; for six days, human creative activity and work can take place, but on the seventh day, we are to stop, reflect on God's goodness, and take rest and pleasure in our doings. Even if one believes (as I do) that the theological motivation for this Sabbath rest has passed away for Christians, the natural need remains. We imitate the Lord who "rested" on the seventh day, "blessed" it, and "hallowed" it as the Sabbath.[33]

Jonathan Sarfati argues that this type of literary interpretation is of recent origin and therefore should be dismissed from consideration, since it was unknown to previous exegetes. He calls it a "bizarre, novel" interpretation and states that it was first introduced by Arie Noordrzij in the year 1924.[34] However, similar commentaries have indeed arisen in previous centuries. For example, the foremost Lithuanian Jewish scholar of the eighteenth century was Rabbi Elijah ben Solomon Zalman (1720-97), better known as the Vilna Gaon. "Known for his greatness in Talmudic and Kabbalistic study, he likewise mastered astronomy, mathematics, and music."[35] His analysis of this chapter is similar to that given above:

> The Vilna Gaon notes that the creations of the first three days and those of the next three days paralleled and complemented one another. Light was created on the first day, and the luminaries were set in place on the fourth. The seas and atmosphere were created on the second day, and aquatic and

bird life were created on the fifth. The dry land and vegetation were created on the third, and populated on the sixth.[36]

And, of course, the division between "form," on the one hand, and the material embodiment of that form in a particular "thing," on the other, dates back to Pythagoras and Plato in the pre-Christian Greek world. There's no real reason a roughly similar idea could not have been expressed by the Hebrew writer of Genesis 1: a division between the "forms" creation took (light, water, sky, land), and the "inhabitants" of those forms (stars, fish, birds, animals, humans). The universe is no longer "without form" and no longer "void" or empty.

In other words, the central idea expressed by the Literary interpretation is simply that *God created everything*—anything that exists in reality is a product of God's creative activity, and thus He receives our glory for all.

(2) The Allegorical interpretation:

Most people are familiar with the idea of allegory, in which the elements and characters of a story actually represent something else besides the story's surface meaning. However, many do not know that Augustine, one of the most important thinkers and writers in the history of Christianity, argued for an allegorical interpretation of Genesis 1.

Given God's eternal and especially *unchanging* nature, Augustine believed that creation had to have occurred in a single timeless moment: "It follows that He [God] does not will first one thing and then another [because that would entail change in God], but that He wills all that He wills simultaneously, in one act, and eternally. He does not repeat his act of will over and over again or will different things at different times."[37] The "days" of creation would then be interpreted as the historical, universal outworking of the creative action God had already accomplished (i.e., before any interactions of matter and space, and therefore before the beginning of what we call "time"). This would remain true even if Augustine were a "Young-Earth" creationist, as he appears to be in some of his other writings.

Also, notice from Augustine that logical arguments, not only scientific, can be advanced against the six-24-hour-days theory of creation. (This logical argument is what Jonathan Sarfati refers to as "Augustine's error."[38]) For Augustine, the number six has symbolic importance, which makes the writer of Genesis use "six days" of creation to present six pictures of what God actually accomplished instantaneously.

In moving toward his allegorical interpretation of Genesis, presented in Book 13 of the *Confessions*, Augustine points out that many interpretations of the first chapters of Genesis already existed in his day. As mentioned, he argues that the "literal" interpretation of six 24-hour days could not be accurate, since that interpretation would require that God exist in time and that God undergo change in his will, actions, duration in time, and so on.[39] Therefore, other interpretations are not only possible, but actually beneficial: "O my God, Light of my eyes in darkness, since I believe in these commandments and confess them to be true with all my heart, how can it harm me that it should be possible to interpret these words in several ways, all of which may yet be true? How can it harm me if I understand the writer's meaning in a different sense from that in which another understands it?"[40]

To those who would say, "Well, but the writer of Genesis certainly did not intend an allegorical meaning to the creation story," Augustine responds:

> But the truths which those words contain appear to different inquirers in a different light, and of all the meanings that they can bear which of us can lay his finger upon one and say that it is what Moses had in mind and what he meant us to understand by his words? Can he say this with as much confidence as he would say that what Moses wrote is the truth, whether he had that particular meaning in mind or another? . . . . When so many meanings, all of them acceptable as true, can be extracted from the words that Moses wrote, do you not see how foolish it is to make a bold assertion that one in particular is the one he had in mind? Do you not see how foolish it is to enter into mischievous arguments which are an offense against that very charity for the sake of which he wrote every one of the words that we are trying to explain?[41]

It strikes me that if all readers were to accept Augustine's counsel in this excerpt, this chapter I am writing would be unnecessary. All of us can make the bold assertion that Genesis reveals God as the Creator of the universe. Beyond that, can we be equally bold in asserting that our particular interpretation of Genesis is the correct one? As Christian writer Fred Heeren puts it, "The *fact* of creation is critical, but God's timing is not something to break fellowship over."[42] Are the seemingly endless disputes over the timetable of creation "mischievous arguments" which offend against "charity"?

After the argument of Books 11-12, Augustine gives his own interpretation of Genesis 1 in Book 13. I am not going to recapitulate his reasons for each interpretation, since they are easily discoverable by the reader, but merely summarize his conclusions:

- God creates the "heaven and earth," which stand for both spiritual and corporeal creatures.
- "Light and darkness" = good souls and wicked souls. The original "Let there be light" also includes the creation of angels, the beings of light.
- The firmament over the waters = the sacred Scriptures and their writers.
- The sea = the tearful bitterness (salt water) of the lives of the unsaved.
- The dry land = the saved rising out of their tearful bitterness.
- Grass, trees, fruit = the good works rising out of the saved.

- Sun, moon, stars = wisdom, knowledge, spiritual gifts.
- Adam's "living" soul = the restraining of carnal passions in the soul.
- Sea creatures = the great works of the saints as witnesses to the world.
- The "image of God," "dominion" = the rational powers of judgment.
- The multiplication of sea creatures = physical signs and miracles (for the unsaved).
- The multiplication of humans = the spread of rational thought (for the saved).
- The seventh-day rest = eternal life with God.
- And so on.

Perhaps many will not find Augustine's allegorical interpretation plausible. But perhaps many will. As Augustine himself says, how can it harm us that it should be possible to interpret these words in several ways?

(3) The Scientific Correspondence interpretation:

A variety of interpretations of Genesis 1 might be placed together under the name of "Scientific Correspondence." For example, "Old-Earth" creationism, theistic evolutionism, and Hugh Ross's "progressive creationism," all would consider biblical teachings on creation to "correspond" to the findings of science. Perhaps the most common form of Scientific Correspondence is the "Day / Age" concept, in which the "days" of creation stand for "ages" of varying lengths—perhaps of millions or even billions of years. Protestant apologists Norman Geisler and Ron Brooks state this view succinctly:

> [T]here are many Creationists who argue for an old earth. Biblically, this position is that the word for *day* is used for more than twenty-four hours even in Genesis 2:4. . . . Scientifically, this view does not require any novel theories to explain the evidence. . . . We have watched star explosions that happened billions of years ago, but if the universe is not billions of years old, then we are seeing light from stars that never existed—because they would have died before Creation. Why would God deceive us with the evidence? The old earth view seems to fit the evidence better and causes no problem with the Bible.[43]

In fact, this view seems so obvious to some proponents of it that Hugh Ross professes he was honestly stunned at discovering his ideas were controversial to many Christians:

> This was my first exposure to the raging storm of the creation-day controversy. . . . The solidity of the scientific evidence for both Earth's

origin (a few billion years ago) and the universe's beginning (a few more billion years ago) raised not a moment's doubt about the necessity of a Creator. Nor did it cause me concern when I first read the Genesis 1 creation account. It honestly did not register with me that anyone could or would see a need to propose that the earth and universe are only a few thousands of years old or that the Genesis days are consecutive calendar days.[44]

Perhaps it is redundant to again point out here that a number of readings of Genesis 1 besides the literal are held by equally committed and devout believers.

One of the more detailed recent attempts to coalesce billions of years of universal history into the "days" of Genesis 1 is given in the book *The Science of God*, by Gerald L. Schroeder. While there are many books and writers we could examine to find examples of Scientific Correspondence interpretations of Genesis, we'll use Schroeder's work due to its clarity and accessibility. For each consecutive day of Genesis 1, Schroeder gives the biblical description (BD) and the corresponding scientific description (SD), and I will summarize these in order:

- Day 1: (BD)—Light is created. (SD)—The Big Bang marks the creation of the universe; light literally breaks free as electrons bond to atomic nuclei; galaxies form. This "day" covers roughly eight billion years.
- Day 2: (BD)—The firmament of heaven is created. (SD)—The Milky Way and our own sun form. This "day" covers roughly four billion more years.
- Day 3: (BD)—Oceans, dry land, and plants are created on earth. (SD)—Liquid water appears on earth, followed by bacteria and photosynthetic algae (plant life). This "day" covers roughly two billion more years.
- Day 4: (BD)—The sun, moon, and stars are created. (SD)—Photosynthesis produces an oxygen-rich atmosphere, which becomes transparent. Were there any terrestrial observers, the stars would have been visible for the first time. This "day" covers roughly one billion more years.
- Day 5: (BD)—Animal life appears in water and the air. (SD)—The first multicellular animals appear; basic animals appear in the waters; winged insects appear. This "day" covers roughly a half-billion more years.
- Day 6: (BD)—Land animals, mammals, and humans are created. (SD)—A massive die-off occurs; the earth is re-populated by land animals, hominids, and then humans. This "day" covers roughly 250 million years.[45]

To this summary I might add: According to our best knowledge today, the great urban civilizations with written histories and thus cultural transmission of our true humanity begin to emerge in the Middle East—*about 6,000 years ago*. At the conclusion of Day 6, in other words.

Earlier I asked the question, "Can one be a believing, biblically-oriented Christian and still reject the literal six-day account of Creation?" I hope I've shown at least three reasons why I think the answer is yes. And, in case anyone wants to know, my own view of Genesis 1 is closest to the Literary interpretation, given in section (1) above. I gave it the least discussion space, in an attempt to be fair in presenting the other views.

Do you hold a different interpretation of the creation story than any of those I've listed here? Or, after having read this chapter, do you hold more strongly than ever to the idea of a literal six-day creation?

In either case, that's fine with me; my purpose is not division, but unity. Do you believe in a Creator? So do I. So do all the other Christians and Jews I've discussed in this section. As the Creeds state, "We believe in God the Father Almighty, Creator of heaven and earth." In order to preserve a biblically-oriented union with our fellow Christians, that sentence is really all we need to believe about Creation. And that's enough.

Questions for Reflection:

1. In this chapter, we've looked at four interpretations of Genesis 1: the literal interpretation; the literary interpretation; the allegorical interpretation; the scientific correspondence interpretation. Which is closest to your own view? Why?

2. If you did not believe in a literal six days of creation and someone told you that, because of this, you were not a "good" Christian or not a "Bible-believing" Christian, how would you respond?

3. If you did not believe in a literal six days of creation and someone asked you if you believed the Bible was true, how would you respond?

4. Suppose we were at a football game together and I commented to you, "That halfback on the other team is fast as lightning." Is what I said true?

5. Will we meet up again in the next chapter?

References

1) Genesis 1:1.

2) Genesis 1:27.

3) Psalm 19:1.

4) John Wilson, "Unintelligent Debate." *Christianity Today.* Sept. 2004: 64-65.

5) Ken Ham, *Why Won't They Listen?* 2nd printing. Green Forest, Arkansas: Master Books, 2003: 147.

6) Henry M. Morris, *Many Infallible Proofs: Evidences for the Christian Faith.* El Cajon, California: Master Books, 1974. 9th printing, 1988: 273.

7) 1 Cor. 14:33.

8) J.R. Porter, "Creation." *The Oxford Guide to Ideas and Issues of the Bible.* Edited by Bruce M. Metzger and Michael D. Coogan. Oxford: Oxford University Press, 2001: 113.

9) Phil Dowe, "Augustine and the Interpretation of Genesis." utas.edu.au/docs/focus/ May97/augustine.

10) For example, Jonathan Sarfati, *Refuting Compromise.* Green Forest, Arkansas: Master Books, 2004: 35-ff.

11) Mark Noll, "The Evangelical Mind Today." *First Things.* October 2004: 34-35.

12) Alan Lacey, "Naturalism." *The Oxford Companion to Philosophy.* Edited by Ted Honderich. Oxford: Oxford University Press, 1995: 604.

13) Ken Ham, "A Young Earth—It's Not the Issue!" answersingenesis.org.

14) Titus 1:2.

15) Harry L. Poe and Jimmy H. Davis, *Science and Faith: An Evangelical Dialogue.* Nashville: Broadman and Holman, 2000: 101.

16) "Creation." *The Oxford Dictionary of the Christian Church.* 2nd edition. Edited by F.L. Cross and E.A. Livingstone. Oxford: Oxford University Press, 1989: 357.

17) Michael Shermer, "Is Design a Good Idea for Science?" Opening Debate, "Design and Its Critics" conference. Concordia University, Mequon, Wisconsin. June 22, 2000.

18) Other key figures in the Intelligent Design debate are William Dembski and Phillip Johnson, whose works I recommend for anyone interested in more than my too-brief summary.

19) Michael Behe, *Darwin's Black Box: The Biochemical Challenge to Evolution.* New York: The Free Press, 1996: 192-93.

20) Klaus Dose, "The Origin of Life: More Questions Than Answers." *Interdisciplinary Science Review* 13 (1998): 348. Quoted in Lee Strobel, *The Case for Faith*: 150 (see next footnote).

21) Quoted in Lee Strobel, *The Case for Faith.* Grand Rapids, Michigan: Zondervan, 2000: 152.

22) Quoted in Donald A. Yerxa, "Phillip Johnson and the Origins of the Intelligent Design Movement, 1977-1991." *Perspectives on Science and Christian Faith.* March 2002: 48.

23) Robert C. Koons, "Do Anthropic Coincidences Require Explanation?" Lectures 11 and 12. leaderu.com.

24) Stephen M. Barr, "Anthropic Coincidences." *First Things.* June / July 2001: 20.

25) Hugh Ross, "Design and the Anthropic Principle." reasons.org.

26) Alan Guth, "Inflationary Universe: A Possible Solution to the Horizon and Flatness Problems." *Physical Review D* 23 (1981): 348.

27) Taken from Gerald L. Schroeder's *The Science of God: The Convergence of Scientific and Biblical Wisdom.* New York: The Free Press, 1997: 5.

28) "Famous Atheist Now Believes in God." Associated Press, Dec. 9, 2004. abcnews.com.

29) Roy Abraham Varghese, "Does Modern Science Undermine Atheism?" *The American Enterprise* April / May 2005: 22.

30) A good recent summary of Intelligent Design findings in many fields is Lee Strobel's *The Case for a Creator.* Grand Rapids, Michigan: Zondervan, 2004.

31) Jonathan Sarfati, *Refuting Compromise*: 26.

32) Genesis 1:2.

33) Exodus 20:8-11.

34) Jonathan Sarfati, *Refuting Compromise*: 136.

35) "Great Leaders of Our People: Vilna Gaon." ou.org/about/judaism/rabbis/gaon.

36) *The Chumash.* Commentary written by Rabbi Nosson Scherman. 11th edition. The Artscroll Series: The Stone Edition. Brooklyn: Mesorah Publications, 2001: 5.

37) Augustine, *Confessions.* Book 12, Chapter 15. Translated by R.S. Pine-Coffin. New York: Penguin Books, 1961: 290.

38) Jonathan Sarfati, *Refuting Compromise*: 118.

39) *Confessions.* Book 11, Chapters 4-13.

40) *Confessions.* Book 12, Chapter 18: 295-96.

41) *Confessions.* Book 12, Chapters 24 and 26: 300, 303.

42) Fred Heeren, *Show Me God: What the Message from Space Is Telling Us About God. Volume 1: Wonders That Witness to the Bible's Truth.* Wheeling, Illinois: Searchlight Publications, 1995: 156.

43) Norman Geisler and Ron Brooks, *When Skeptics Ask: A Handbook on Christian Evidences.* 6th printing. Grand Rapids, Michigan: Baker Books, 2001: 230.

44) Hugh Ross, *A Matter of Days: Resolving a Creation Controversy.* Colorado Springs: Navpress, 2004: 14-15.

45) Gerald L. Schroeder, *The Science of God: The Convergence of Scientific and Biblical Wisdom.* New York: The Free Press, 1997: 66-ff.

Chapter 4: What Does "Inspired" Mean?

"In what sense does the Bible 'present' the Jonah story as 'historical'? Of course it doesn't say 'This is fiction,' but then neither does our Lord say that the Unjust Judge, Good Samaritan, or Prodigal Son are fiction. . . . How does a denial, a doubt, of their historicity lead logically to a similar denial of New Testament miracles? Supposing (as I think is the case) that sound critical reading revealed different *kinds* of narrative in the Bible, surely it would be illogical to suppose that these different kinds should all be read in the same way?"—from a famous Protestant Christian writer.

"We must say that if [evangelical Christians] are to be evangelicals, we must not compromise our view of Scripture. There is no use in evangelicalism seeming to get larger and larger, if at the same time appreciable parts of evangelicalism are getting soft at that which is the central core—namely, the Scriptures. . . . We must say most lovingly but clearly: evangelicalism is not consistently evangelical unless there is a line drawn between those who take a full view of Scripture and those who do not."—from a famous Protestant Christian writer.

"All Scripture is given by inspiration of God"—2 Timothy 3:16.

How Should We Read the Bible?

Through the years, I've heard many Christians say something like the following: "The Bible should be read first of all literally, the same way we'd read a newspaper or a textbook. If we read it in any other way than the literal and historical, that reading should be a last option, only taken if the text is impossible to accept in the literal sense." However, in this chapter, I plan to argue that holding this interpretive stance is not absolutely necessary in order to remain a faithful Christian. Believing that the Bible is inspired by God does not necessarily require one to believe that every part of the Bible is equally literal and historical.

Christians (myself included) believe that the Bible as we have it today is God's inspired Word, revealed supernaturally to its many writers, infallible in its teachings and inerrant if read in the way its original writers intended it to be read. However, a great deal is contained in that final phrase. In what ways did

their original writers intend the various books of the Bible to be read? Is every part of the Bible intended to be read as equally historical? Is the Bible no longer inspired if parts of it are read as inspired story rather than inspired history? If God's Word is "His Story," does that necessarily mean it is all also "history"? If it's not all history, does that make parts of the Bible a mythtake?

The "inerrancy" of the Bible is a denomination-splitting issue in some parts of the Church today, especially in evangelical Protestant circles. Here's a definition of the term taken from an evangelical Protestant theological dictionary:

> Inerrancy is the view that when all the facts become known, they will demonstrate that the Bible in its original autographs [the original manuscripts of the Bible] and correctly interpreted is entirely true and never false in all it affirms, whether that relates to doctrine or ethics or to the social, physical, or life sciences.[1]

With this definition I have no major problems—but I do have a difference. The difference is not one of definition, but one of emphasis. Earlier I mentioned my belief that the Bible is "inerrant if read in the way its original writers intended it to be read." So first of all I would bring out two words in the above definition: The Bible is entirely true and never false in all it affirms if it is *correctly interpreted*. Secondly, I would argue that some parts of the Bible commonly interpreted as literal history are not so meant to be interpreted.

Many Christians, of course, disagree (to put it mildly). Take another look at the two long quotes with which this chapter opens. They are both from leading twentieth-century Christian writers and apologists, the first from C.S. Lewis,[2] the second from Francis Schaeffer.[3] In his book *No Final Conflict*, Schaeffer explicitly argues that the Bible, in order to be accepted as truly inspired by God and truthful, must be accepted as propositional, historical, and strictly factual; this is what he calls the "full view" and the "strong view" of Scripture. "The issue is whether the Bible gives propositional truth (that is, truth that may be stated in propositions) where it touches history and the cosmos, and this all the way back to pre-Abrahamic history . . ." He brings up this pre-Abrahamic portion of the Bible (Genesis 1-11) again a page later:

> It should be noted in studying the book of Genesis that there is no literary distinction between the sections dealing with history and the sections dealing with the cosmos, on the one hand, and religious subjects, on the other hand.[4]

Later in this chapter, we'll look at various criteria for measuring the "literary distinction" between statements intended historically and those intended otherwise. For now, what we need to notice is that Schaeffer would vehemently disagree with Lewis's "fictional" reading of parts of the Old Testament, although he quotes Lewis throughout his works, including in the book from which these excerpts are taken.

So we are left with the question: Which is the view we lesser lights should adopt? Which is the "correct" Christian interpretive stance? Is Lewis right or is Schaeffer? Or (my point in this chapter) could equally Bible-believing Christians differ on this issue?

Upon first reading of his works, medieval Catholic philosopher Thomas Aquinas would seem in agreement with Schaeffer's viewpoint: The "spiritual explanation" of biblical passages, he says, "must always be based on the literal."[5] In the *Summa Theologica*, he maintains the "literal" sense of Scripture as primary:

> [N]othing false can underlie the literal sense of Scripture. . . . [T]he parabolic sense is contained in the literal sense. . . . Nothing that is necessary to faith is contained under the spiritual sense which is not openly conveyed by the literal sense elsewhere. [In the *Summa* itself, the sentences actually appear in reverse order from the way quoted here, but their general context does not change.][6]

Aquinas definitely cautions us that all theological discussions must be firmly grounded on the literal sense of the Bible, not speculative "spiritualizing" of the text. In fact, he sounds positively Protestant—even evangelical—when he warns, "Only the canonical Scriptures are normative for faith."[7] Probably Schaeffer himself would have said it no differently.

Furthermore, this seems a good time to bring up the question of the miraculous in biblical narratives. The alert reader will see that whether or not a biblical story contains the miraculous has absolutely nothing to do with whether or not the story is to be taken as literal history. When Jesus heals a blind man, we may "spiritualize" the text all we want: "Yes, I too once was (spiritually) blind, but now I (spiritually) see." But Aquinas (and Lewis and Schaeffer) would insist first of all on reading the text as presented. If it is presented as a literal, historical account, then the healing was a literal, historical healing, even if it was also a miracle—in other words, if we'd been there with a video camera, we could have recorded it on film. It wasn't a "metaphorical" or "allegorical" healing if not presented as metaphor or allegory. The reader may certainly *disbelieve* the account if he or she so chooses, but the reader is not free to read the account as "non-historical" simply because of anti-miraculous presuppositions brought to the text. Let's read the Bible as it is written.

On the other hand, is the entire Bible written as history? Aquinas himself is certainly not a "literalistic" reader of the Bible. Our key to understanding what he actually asserts here in the *Summa* is provided in the very same passage, as he defines what he means by the "literal sense" of Scripture:

> Since the literal sense is that which the author intends, and since the author of Holy Writ is God, Who by one act comprehends all things by His

intellect, it is not unfitting . . . if, even according to the literal sense, one word in Holy Writ should have several senses.[8]

For Aquinas, therefore, a "literal" reading of the Scriptures is a reading *according to the intention of the divine Author* (here he makes no mention of the human authors, the instruments of God's inspiration, but this does not change the force of his argument). So if God intends part of the Bible as history, a "literal" reading would read that part as inspired history. On the other hand, if God intends parts of the Bible as parable, or metaphor, as non-historical or even (to use Lewis's word) "fiction," then a "literal" reading of the Bible would read it in precisely these ways: as parable, as metaphor, even as fiction if necessary.

Further, these non-historical parts of the Bible would be *just as inspired as the historical,* and just as binding upon biblical believers. If, as C.S. Lewis implies, the book of Jonah may be read as "fiction," that does not change at all its status as both inspired and normative. As stated earlier, the Bible stands alone, revealed supernaturally to its many writers, both infallible and inerrant. But "inerrant" here means the Bible is without error if and only if read in the way intended by its divine Author. This idea is more fully stated by William A. Dowd in *The Catholic Encyclopedia Dictionary*:

> All error is excluded from the Bible since God is its principal Author; if it contained error, God Himself would be responsible for that error, but this is impossible because of His infinite knowledge and truthfulness. Hence everything in the original books is infallibly true *in the sense intended by the author* [emphasis added].[9]

"So what's history and what's not?" some readers may question at this point. "How can we always tell what God intends as historical and what He intends as non-historical? This seems to leave too much up to the judgment of the reader—it's better just to accept everything in the Bible as equally historical and be done with it."

To this objection I respond, I hope in charity and gentleness: If we are going to adopt this more literalistic view, what Schaeffer calls the "strong" and "full" view of Scripture, we really need to have better reasons to do so than just our habits of laziness in study. Just because our Bible reading would be made more difficult by taking into account the various intentions of the Author is no reason not to do it. In fact, would not this approach make our Bible reading more full and rich and rewarding in every way? And recognizing the difference between poetic metaphor and literal history is actually not that difficult; in fact, the simplest of Bible readers have been doing it quite successfully for centuries.

The Anglican Lewis and the Catholic Aquinas are not the only ones who make the case for this type of interpretive stance. In an interview, evangelical Charles Colson, formerly of Watergate notoriety but now better known as a Christian writer and the founder of Prison Fellowship, puts forward almost exactly the same idea:

The Bible is not like any other book, but you have to read it like any other book. Parables are parables. Poetry is poetry. Metaphors are metaphors. Allegories are allegories. Where you have to be careful . . . is reading a didactic teaching as didactic teaching, reading historical accounts as clearly historical accounts, and reading parables as parables. When it says that the heavens declare the glory of God, well, we know that the heavens don't speak. We use the same kinds of expression in modern American language. . . . We say that the sun rises. But the sun doesn't rise, obviously. We know that. But that's a figure of speech. And the Bible is replete with figures of speech that people could understand, and they have to be read as figures of speech.[10]

Let me offer three examples to help us understand Colson's point, one taken from our own contemporary speech, two from the Bible. If you ask your favorite aunt how she's doing and she responds, "I've been climbing the walls lately," how do you react? Do you picture her scaling the curtains in the dining room? Do you assume she is in a rock-climbing group and has been practicing indoors? No, of course not; you understand exactly what she is saying, and you sympathize.

Now suppose someone were to say to you, "I'm a firm believer in the inerrancy of favorite aunts. If you don't believe your aunt has been literally 'climbing the walls' lately, you are not a true believer in the Word of Aunt. Either you take what she says literally or you don't believe her at all." With this example, we readily see the silliness of trying to apply "inerrancy" to any textual expression *without taking into consideration the author's intent.* If we don't understand the author's real meaning in a text, what's the point of arguing whether or not the text is "inerrant"? Remember that part of the definition of the "inerrancy" of the Bible requires that the Bible be "correctly interpreted." A strictly literalistic interpretation will miss the true meaning in many cases and will itself lead us into errant beliefs.

For example, the prophet Isaiah proclaims that the Lord shall "gather together the dispersed of Judah from the four corners of the earth."[11] The "literal" meaning of the "four corners of the earth"—i.e., the meaning *as intended*—is simply "all the earth." Any attempt to make the "four corners" of the earth mean anything excessively literalistic will cause misinterpretation, since the earth has no "corners."

So far, so good (perhaps). However, here's a somewhat more controversial example from the Bible: If you read of the Lord as saying, "They shall see the Son of man coming in the clouds of heaven with power and great glory,"[12] do you check the weather outside? Or do you check the other scriptural passages describing the Lord "coming in the clouds of heaven" to see what this language might otherwise mean apart from the literalistic interpretation?

"Now wait a minute. I take that passage literally, as I take all the Bible," you might say. But first of all, we are not at liberty to take the passage literally if that is not what the Author meant by it—or better, as Aquinas would have it, to truly take the passage "literally" would mean to find out precisely what the

Author *did* mean by it, and read it in that way. How is "cloud" imagery used in connection with a "coming of the Lord" elsewhere in the Bible? Is it a metaphor or is it a scientific description of atmospheric conditions? In order to grasp the *meaning* of an expression, we must also grasp the *mode* of the expression. Does a sunny day rule out the coming of the Lord?

Secondly, once we do begin to read the Bible in this more probing way, we will begin to see the beneficial results in our own devotional and spiritual lives, as the Word becomes more rich and rewarding to us—and even more *understandable.*

Here's a remarkable paradox: When we do not insist on reading every single passage of the Bible as equally literal and historical, we can actually begin to understand more fully what the Bible is *literally saying.* As the Bible itself declares, God has spoken to us through His human vessels at many different times, in many different ways.[13] A more complete appreciation of God's different ways of speaking will develop in us a more complete appreciation of God's Word as well.

Questions for Reflection:

1. In this section, I've argued that the notion of biblical "inerrancy" must take into consideration the types of writing found in the Bible, and the authors' intentions in writing. What do you think of this idea? Do you think it unnecessarily complicates the issue?

2. Is the Bible no longer inspired if parts of it are read as inspired "story" rather than inspired "history"? Could you explain your answer?

3. Are Jesus' parables (such as "The Good Samaritan") factual accounts of events that literally happened? If not, are the parables "true"? Are they "inspired"?

4. "Believing that the Bible is inspired by God does not necessarily require one to believe that every part of the Bible is equally literal and historical," I wrote in this section. Many Christians would think of this sentence as "watering down" biblical belief, or even as an expression of outright denial of belief in the inspired Word. Obviously, I would disagree. Can you reconstruct the reasons I would disagree?

5. Suppose you are at a religious service and hear a minister say the following two sentences: "We know the Bible is the true Word of God, true all the way from the first word of Genesis to the last word of Revelation. It is completely historical and

literal, and anyone who says anything different is trying to tear down your faith in the Holy Scriptures." What would be (1) your first response? (2) your response to the first sentence? (3) your response to the second sentence?

6. I would agree with the minister's first sentence in Question 5, but not the second. How does this compare with your response to that question? Do you personally think this chapter is an attempt to tear down your faith in the inspiration, authority, and truthfulness of the Bible? (By the way, if you feel within yourself that your faith in the inspiration, authority, and truthfulness of the Bible *has* in fact been harmed by your reading of this chapter, then I would put this book away immediately. Don't pick it up again until you sense God's leading or direction to do so. I am not joking—I am completely serious. It is not a put-down or condescension on my part when I say that not everyone will be equally prepared to understand the message I'm trying to get across in this book, and any misunderstanding in these crucial areas could cause actual spiritual harm rather than the help I intend.)

7. As a preview to the next section, ask yourself: "What kinds of tests do I myself use (more or less unconsciously) to decide whether or not a statement is a literal, historical description?" For example, why do we all agree that the stories of Alexander the Great are historical, but the stories of Hercules aren't?

What Makes a Story Historical?

Much of the discussion of the previous section was brought to the attention of the general evangelical Protestant world by a single famous, or infamous, footnote in C.S. Lewis's *Miracles* (my own favorite of all his remarkable books). In fact, the personal letter quoted at the very beginning of this chapter was Lewis's response to a reader's question regarding the following footnote:

> My present view—which is tentative and liable to any amount of correction—would be that just as, on the factual side, a long preparation culminates in God's becoming incarnate as Man, so, on the documentary side, the truth first appears in *mythical* form and then by a long process of condensing or focusing finally becomes incarnate as History. This involves the belief that Myth in general is . . . at its best, a real though unfocused gleam of divine truth falling on human imagination. The Hebrews, like other people, had mythology; but as they were the chosen people so their mythology was the chosen mythology—the mythology chosen by God to be the vehicle of the earliest sacred truths, the first step

in that process which ends in the New Testament where truth has become completely historical. Whether we can ever say with certainty where, in this process of crystallization, any particular Old Testament story falls, is another matter. I take it that the memoirs of David's court come at one end of the scale and are scarcely less historical than St. Mark or Acts; and that the Book of Jonah is at the opposite end.[14]

To professor Corbin Carnell's disconcerted query regarding the rather off-handed reference to the Book of Jonah, Lewis replied, "In what sense does the Bible 'present' the Jonah story as 'historical'? Of course it doesn't say 'This is fiction,' but then neither does our Lord say that the Unjust Judge, Good Samaritan, or Prodigal Son are fiction." He continues:

> How does a denial, a doubt, of their historicity lead logically to a similar denial of New Testament miracles? Supposing (as I think is the case) that sound critical reading revealed different *kinds* of narrative in the Bible, surely it would be illogical to suppose that these different kinds should all be read in the same way?[15]

Notice in these quotes that Lewis takes the New Testament Gospels and Acts as literal, factual history, but asserts that there are "different kinds of narrative" in the Bible, especially in the Old Testament. So before we begin looking at distinctions between history and myth, and how to determine which one we are reading, perhaps we could review the different kinds of narrative (the different "genres," to use the literary term) contained in the Bible.

For example, even a fairly casual reading of the Old Testament reveals instances of the genres of straightforward history, biography, autobiography, law code, prophecy, parable, drama, short story, aphorism, and poetry, as well as lesser known genres such as lament, hymn, allegory, etiology, and fable[16]:

- History—1 and 2 Kings, 1 and 2 Chronicles.
- Biography—Daniel 4.
- Autobiography—most of the books of Ezra and Nehemiah.
- Law code—most of the book of Leviticus.
- Prophecy—Daniel 11-12.
- Parable—Ezekiel 17.
- Drama—the book of Job, whether or not it is historical, is structured as a drama.
- Short story—the book of Jonah, whether or not it is historical, is structured as a short story. (The books of Ruth and of Esther are also structured as short stories. Of course, they are given a historical grounding as well. However, accepting these books historically need not blind us to their other literary qualities.)
- Aphorism—most of the book of Proverbs.
- Poetry—the books of Psalms and of Lamentations.

- Lament—Psalm 137.
- Hymn—Psalms 146-150.
- Allegory—Ezekiel 23.
- Etiology—Esther 9.
- Fable—Judges 9:6-20.

"Surely it would be illogical to suppose that these different kinds should all be read in the same way?" Lewis asks us. Yet part of our difficulty in biblical understanding lies in the fact that often we *do* indeed try to read all these various genres in the same way—the way of a literalistic understanding of them as straightforward history. Earlier I quoted Charles Colson, "The Bible is not like any other book, but you have to read it like any other book." In other words, we need to read the Bible first of all for what it has to say to us in the way it has to say it, as we would read any other book, without presupposing it will all come out like a newspaper account or like a textbook summary. God's different ways of speaking to us in His Word require different interpretive methods on our part.

In their helpful work *Handbook of Christian Apologetics*, Roman Catholic professors and writers Peter Kreeft and Ronald Tacelli list eight basic principles of biblical interpretation. Four of them are relevant here and will serve to summarize our discussion:

1) Use common standards, methods, and approaches; approach the Bible as you would approach any other book, in other words. Let's not assume we already know exactly what the Bible is going to say and exactly how it's going to say it.

2) Read for the author's intended meaning.

3) Interpret a book according to its genre. We wouldn't have the same interpretive presuppositions for poetic metaphor as we would for a law code.

4) Know which stories are historical.[17] If a story is not intended as literal or historical, and we interpret it as such, we do harm to the actual inerrancy of the Bible. In fact, we ourselves introduce error into people's understanding of the Scriptures.

"Sometimes we are tempted to think," says writer Michael J. Christensen, "that God should have penned the Bible Himself and presented it to us fresh from the eternal inkwell on a take-it-or-leave-it basis without any human element affecting its composition or obscuring its divine light. Life would have been so much simpler, we imagine. . . . But there is nothing to be gained by wishful thinking."[18] Because God has chosen to reveal his Word in the way He has chosen to reveal it, we must accept his methods as best, even though they may require extra interpretive effort on the part of faithful readers.

"Well, now we're back to my original question, the one you dismissed in the previous section," you might interject. "How can we always tell what God intends as historical and what He intends as non-historical? You yourself brought this up in the last 'Questions for Reflection'—why do we accept the stories about Alexander the Great as historical, but not the stories of Hercules? Okay, I'll bite. Why do we? What's history and what's not?"

What is history and what is not? At the risk of (further) irritating the reader, I'm going to ask you to think about this for yourself. What do you look for in a historical account? If you answer, "I look for specific names, places, and dates," I could give you specific names and places and approximate dates for the adventures of Tom Sawyer, Becky Thatcher, and Huck Finn—but they're not history, even though we often refer to them by name even as Jesus referred to Jonah by name. Why aren't they historical?

What else do you look for in a historical account? If you answer, "It has to have occurred in reality, which the adventures of Tom Sawyer did not," you're getting closer, but someone could still argue that the adventures of Hercules, as unlikely as they might be, could just possibly have occurred in reality. Who would know?

If you respond, "But the adventures of Hercules were not related by eye-witnesses, and besides that, they have no outside corroboration by anyone except the one who told the story," we are beginning to hit nearer the bull's-eye. Now we're actually coming up with *historical tests*: the criteria by which we decide that one story is literally historical in nature and another isn't.

Let's list what we have so far, and I'll add a bit more:

- Ideally, in order to qualify as history, the story should be related by an eyewitness. More than one eyewitness would be even better.
- If the story is not related by an eyewitness, the next best storyteller would be a contemporary of the event, or at least someone close to being a contemporary.
- It would also be advantageous to have the story, or features of the story, corroborated by someone not directly connected to the action or to the storyteller.
- How to tell if something occurs "in reality"? Of course, archeological evidence would be a crucial help here, but at the very least, the event should produce *definable consequences* in the lives of those surrounding the event.

These criteria spell out in some detail what we've already considered, and also define a bit more what it might mean for something to occur "in reality." Notice, for example, that the adventures of Tom Sawyer do not satisfy any of these historical tests, and therefore we can conclude that they did not occur in reality. Now let me give just two more criteria which might also be helpful:

- It would help to establish historicity if there are some minor variations in the different accounts of the same story.
- It would help to establish historicity if there are some internally damaging details in the story.

"What?" you might be thinking. "Wouldn't these criteria harm, rather than help, the case for historicity in a story?" Really, though, they are a help and not a harm. To take the first: If all witnesses to an event told verbatim the same account of that event, no matter their varying perspectives, abilities, educational levels, social backgrounds, and so on, we'd definitely suspect something was fishy. I would tend to think the story had been prepared either before or after the event, and all the more so as the different accounts became more and more word-for-word identical.

The second is more difficult to explain, especially since we tend to prize internal consistency in a story. But let's think of it this way: If someone tells a story in which some of the internal details are damaging to the credibility of the story, the only logical motive that person would have for including those details is that they are true. For example, in the Gospels, the first witnesses to Jesus' resurrection are women. In first-century Judaism, this detail would be quite damaging; the testimony of women was considered without value, and women were not even allowed to testify in court. Why would the Gospel writers, three of whom were Jewish, include this account unless it was true, especially considering that they were specifically trying to convince readers of the reality of the Resurrection? As C.S. Lewis concludes, "The evangelists [Matthew, Mark, Luke, and John] have the first great characteristic of honest witnesses: they mention facts which are, at first sight, damaging to their main contention."[19] So these "internally damaging details" actually do help to establish the historicity of a narrative.

Now that we have some historical criteria in hand, let's examine three stories, two from the Bible and one not, to consider the different categories into which various stories might be placed. Do the stories of (1) Jesus in the Gospels, (2) Adam and Eve in Genesis, and (3) Hercules in Greek mythology, all satisfy these criteria? Could all these stories be considered literal history as we go through these criteria one by one? Here's the first:

- In order to qualify as history, the story should be related by an eyewitness. More than one eyewitness would be even better.

(1) Jesus in the Gospels: Yes, the Gospels satisfy this criterion. In fact, the Gospel writers make it a point to highlight their eyewitness involvement in the

story.[20] Luke is not an eyewitness, but bases his account on eyewitness reports.[21] Paul mentions over 500 eyewitnesses of Jesus after the Resurrection, "most of whom are still alive," as he puts it.[22]

(2) Adam and Eve in Genesis: No. How could there be eyewitnesses to God's creation of the universe?

(3) Hercules in Greek mythology: No.

- If the story is not related by an eyewitness, the next best storyteller would be a contemporary of the event, or at least someone close to being a contemporary.

(1) Jesus in the Gospels: Yes. See remark on Luke, above. Also, it is possible that John Mark, the author of Mark's Gospel, inserts himself into the story at the point he becomes an actual eyewitness.[23] Luke does the same thing in the book of Acts.[24]

(2) Adam and Eve in Genesis: No.

(3) Hercules in Greek mythology: No.

- The story, or features of the story, should be corroborated by someone not directly connected to the action or to the storyteller.

(1) Jesus in the Gospels: Yes (Jesus' life and the life of the early Christian Church are mentioned in Tacitus, Josephus, Justin Martyr, the Babylonian Talmud, and so on).

(2) Adam and Eve in Genesis: No.

(3) Hercules in Greek mythology: No.

- How to tell if something occurs "in reality"? Of course, archeological evidence would be a crucial help here, but at the very least, the event should produce *definable consequences* in the lives of those surrounding the event.

(1) Jesus in the Gospels: Definitely yes—the transformed lives of the early disciples, to the point they were willing to accept death rather than deny the Resurrection, all the way up to the existence of the worldwide Church today, are consequences of the historical nature of the Gospels.

(2) Adam and Eve in Genesis: Yes. The story of the Garden of Eden tells the story of humanity's glorious creation in God's image and our inglorious Fall. According to Genesis, we humans after the Fall are alienated from God, alienated from Nature, and alienated from each other, all of which we can readily see are true; further, each of us contains a deep inner tendency to sinful wrongdoing (a feature of Original Sin, part of the Fall) along with a deep inner shame and guilty knowledge that we were not created thus (as the *Imago Dei*, part of the Creation). All we have to do is look within ourselves and throughout human history to see that the story of humanity's Fall is accurate.

(3) Hercules in Greek mythology: No definable consequences in history.

- It would help to establish historicity if there are some minor variations in the different accounts of the same story.

(1) Jesus in the Gospels: Yes. The variations, particularly in the Gospel of John, are well known. For example, in a story of healing, one Gospel mentions two blind men, while another Gospel only mentions one.[25] This is explainable (one Gospel mentions both men, while the other only mentions the more vocal of the two); it is not a contradiction, but it is a variation.

(2) Adam and Eve in Genesis: Yes—compare the account of Creation in Genesis 1 with that in Genesis 2.

(3) Hercules in Greek mythology: Yes. The many retellings of the stories of Hercules do contain minor variations.

- It would help to establish historicity if there are some internally damaging details in the story.

(1) Jesus in the Gospels: Yes—the women's testimony already discussed, along with others such as Jesus' lowly birth, shameful death, and so on. These are certainly not characteristics of the Messiah the first-century Jews thought would arrive on the scene, the great Warrior King they eagerly expected. Also, the Gospel writers did not appear to take any pains to make themselves "look good" throughout their narratives, presenting only their best faces; in fact, quite the opposite is often true.

(2) Adam and Eve in Genesis: No.

(3) Hercules in Greek mythology: Yes—in the stories, a constant stress is placed on Hercules' erratic temper, his crucial heroic flaw.

As we take all these together, it seems that three distinct categories begin to emerge. The first I would call *non-history*. The stories of Hercules would fall easily into this category: There are no eyewitnesses to the stories, no contemporary tellers, no outside corroboration, and not even any definable historical consequences. These stories are clearly not intended to be read as literal history.

The second category is more difficult. What about an event with no eyewitnesses, no contemporary tellers, and no outside corroboration, but with definite historical, anthropological (in the sense of *anthropos logos*, the study of the human person), psychological, and spiritual consequences? We can tell historically that the Creation and Fall must have occurred; however, we cannot tell by our historical criteria that they had to have occurred exactly as told in Genesis 1-3. If, of course, we believe that the events *did* occur literally as described, that's not a problem, as long as we understand that the story of Adam and Eve as it stands is substantially different from the stories we typically accept as "literal history." I would refer to this story as *non-literal history*; in other words, the Creation and Fall are facts of the world we live in, part of our human make-up. However, whether or not the Creation and Fall occurred literally and historically as described in Genesis is beyond our knowledge.

We now have the categories of "non-history" and "non-literal history"; this leaves the third category of "literal history," into which I would place the Gospels. I would like you to set aside for a moment any consideration of the many miracles recorded in the Gospels, the perfect Life of Christ, the Resurrection, and so on—because once we set these aside, we quickly see that the *a priori* philosophical objection to the miraculous is virtually the only reason for objecting to the Gospels as history. If we used the same basic techniques for reading the Gospels as we would for reading any other ancient historical narrative, we would immediately see that the Gospels have far more manuscript evidence, satisfy far more historical criteria, and are far more rooted in their known historical context than any other text of comparable age. If it were not for the miraculous events of the Gospels, we would unhesitatingly accept them as models of sound ancient history:

> [I]n order for the four Evangelists' representations of Jesus to be convincing, they had to match the course of events in his life. . . . [A] fair assessment of the evidence supports a high degree of historicity.[26]

As C.S. Lewis argues, not accepting every part of the Old Testament as equally literal and historical does not really change in any way how one reads the New Testament, which *does* seem to be presented as literal and historical. Thus the New Testament seems to fit into this third category of "literal history" just as readily as, say, Caesar's *Gallic Wars*. (Actually, given the amount of early manuscript evidence for the New Testament compared to that for Caesar's work, the New Testament has a *better* claim on historicity.)

Peter Kreeft succinctly summarizes this discussion:

Many undoubted and universally accepted events in secular history have far less textual evidence than the events in the Gospels. They are written later, longer after the event; and there are fewer copies of them for cross-checking. If it didn't contain anything miraculous, biblical history would be accepted as certainly as secular history.[27]

Could it be that many reject the historicity of the New Testament because the idea of God becoming flesh is still as scandalous as ever, still "foolishness" in the term used by Paul the apostle?[28] Surely, we say, we do not need a God to become human for us! And even if God did so, is it possible that humans as innately good as we are would crucify Him? Surely these stories cannot be objectively factual accounts—so perhaps our spiritual pride might want to insist.

However, there could be other objections to the historical nature of the New Testament; as anthropologist Claude Lévi-Strauss writes, "The problem is: where does mythology end and where does history start?"[29] The next section of this chapter will seek to address the question of the relationship of mythic stories to the New Testament.

Questions for Reflection:

1. I made a distinction between "literal history" and "non-literal history," placing the Gospels in the first category and the story of the Garden of Eden in the second. Does this distinction make sense to you? Do you think of it as a mistake? Why or why not?

2. In this section, this sentence appeared: "In their helpful work *Handbook of Christian Apologetics*, Roman Catholic professors and writers Peter Kreeft and Ronald Tacelli list eight basic principles of biblical interpretation." Are you more likely to accept these principles of biblical interpretation because I identified the writers as Roman Catholics, less likely to accept these principles, or neither? Why do you choose the answer you do?

3. We discussed several "historical tests." What other historical tests would you also include? Did I list any you would have left out? Which ones?

Where Myth and History Meet

Myths may be defined as the legendary but artistic stories setting forth an explanation of the fundamentals of human existence: the mysteries of our origin, our purpose, our meaning in life, and so on.[30] Moreover, myth studies seem to be everywhere nowadays. The two-year college at which I teach offers in its curriculum "Myth and Literature" in addition to the more typical American Lit. and World Lit. courses; a school in a neighboring town not only offers a similar course, but also a basic course in mythology for undergraduates and a course, "Studies in Myth," for the more advanced student. In higher education itself, Northrop Frye's theories of literary analysis by way of myth permeate the atmosphere, or at least the atmosphere with which I am most familiar, that of the English and Humanities departments. On television, we see George Lucas of *Star Wars* fame discussing the influence of myth on his films. Even in the mail this week, all of the book club catalogs I received include sections on myth, usually incorporated into the religion / philosophy / "spirituality" sections.

The popularity of myth studies may be attributed to the fact that ours is a relentlessly questioning age, and myth studies purport to examine the central questions of life itself: Why are matters one way, and not another? What is the ground of our being, the ground of the universe we uneasily inhabit? How can we change our situation, and what is the rationale for doing so? Does the possibility for meaningful change even exist, or is any change just another random dance of atoms in the universal pageant? The twentieth-century philosopher and historian Eric Voegelin posits these questions as the two principal questions of life, the questions of "existence" and "essence":

> The quest for the ground . . . is a constant in all civilizations . . . The quest for the ground has been formulated in two principal questions of metaphysics. The first question is, "Why is there something; why not nothing?" and the second is, "Why is that something as it is, and not different?"[31]

In other words, humans eternally ask the question: What is life's purpose? The recent emphasis on myth studies seems to be another manifestation of that persistent query, since myth *does* appear to organize existence into purposeful categories.

However, so also does the Christian story organize existence and give meaning to life. So one might ask, Is Christianity ultimately just another myth, designed to show us a vision of a world of order under God's control and loving care? Is it merely a legendary but artistic story like the Egyptian story of Osiris, judge of the afterlife? And here's another question, speaking of Osiris: Why do so many mythic tales so uncannily parallel and foreshadow the story of the sacrifice and Resurrection of Christ? Are all these stories to be taken as equally fictional?

Here we reach the central questions regarding the relationship between myth and the Gospels: What is the nature of a mythic story? Can myths be "true" in an artistic sense even if not in a historical sense? And, more importantly: Is this what we mean when we talk about the "truth" of Christianity?

Another way of asking the same question is this: Is the Christian story grounded in a historical reality beyond our myth-telling imaginations? Or is it merely a fundamental, aesthetically powerful "illusion," as Freud calls it—a sort of glorified "picture in the clouds"?

Before we go any further, let me offer a reassurance as to my intentions. As already argued in the previous section, I accept the New Testament as literally historical. I accept all the miracles, the sinless Life, the Crucifixion, the Resurrection, and so on, as having actually happened in reality. However, we Christians should not therefore ignore all the mythic parallels Christianity holds to stories from other pre-Christian cultures, or pretend they do not exist. Neither should we maintain, as some do, that all these stories are some kind of demonic counterfeits designed to distract us from the reality—at least, we should not maintain this when there is a better explanation at hand, as I think there is.

In fact, far from seeing these mythic tales as demonic counterfeits of the story of Redemption, we might see God's revelatory hand in them. As one writer puts it:

> Scattered generously throughout the myths of the ancient world is the strange story of a god who came down from heaven. Some tell of a god who died and rose for the life of man (e.g., Odin, Osiris, and Mesopotamian corn gods). Just as the Garden of Eden story and the Noah's flood story appear in many different cultures, something like the Jesus story does too.
>
> For some strange reason, many people think that this fact—that there are many mythic parallels and foreshadowings of the Christian story—points to the *falsehood* of the Christian story. Actually, the more witnesses tell a similar story, the more likely it is to be *true*. The more foreshadowings we find for an event, the more likely it is that the event will happen.[32]

So we could consider mythic and archetypal patterns in the stories of various cultures as a sort of *praeparatio evangelica*, a preparation for the reality of the Gospel to come, a preparation that loses none of its mythic radiance as it finds itself in historical manifestation. Just because many non-Christians fall off one side of the horse by thinking of Jesus as just another myth without historical validity does not mean we Christians have to fall off the other side, by neglecting and discounting mythic parallels to the Gospel when we find them. As Ernest F. Scott writes:

> In a larger sense the New Testament is to be considered historically. The church has always taken its stand on the great principle that the Word was made flesh, the Divine Life identified with humanity. But the implications of this truth used never to be fully grasped. It was assumed that the revelation broke in suddenly, and had nothing in common with anything that had gone before. We now recognize that although it was new it wove itself naturally into the existing life of the world. The forms in which it found expression had been prepared for it by an age-long process of development. Criticism . . . now takes full account of this historical preparation. . . . For centuries before Christ men had been "feeling after

God if haply they might find Him," and the new revelation attached itself
to what was noblest and best in the world's earlier thought.[33]

To better understand this *praeparatio evangelica* by way of analogy, we
might think of universal archetypes and mythic patterns as a sort of "glove." A
glove—no matter how closely it resembles a real hand—is not the hand itself.
However, if not for that close resemblance to the hand, the glove would lose its
point, its meaning. Similarly, myth (in a Christian view) must bear a close
resemblance to the (Christian) reality. As the living reality of the hand fills the
glove and fulfills the glove's purpose with its embodiment of the glove's
pattern, so Christ fills and fulfills the mythic pattern: "Surely the history of the
human mind hangs together better if you suppose that all this was the first
shadowy approach of something whose reality came with Christ."[34] Like a hand
slipping into a carefully prepared glove, the historical reality of Christ perfectly
fulfills the mythic tales, the preparation, pointing toward Him, just as in a
different context He perfectly fulfills the Old Testament prophecies pointing
more accurately and specifically toward Him.

In his autobiographical *Surprised by Joy*, C.S. Lewis maintains this union of
myth and fact in Christ: "If ever a myth had become fact, had been incarnated, it
would be just like this. . . . [T]he myth must have become fact; the Word, flesh;
God, man."[35] He explains himself more fully elsewhere:

> As myth transcends thought, Incarnation transcends myth. The heart of
> Christianity is a myth which is also a fact. The old myth of the Dying God,
> *without ceasing to be myth*, comes down from the heavens of legend and
> imagination to the earth of history. It *happens*—at a particular date, in a
> particular place, followed by definable historical consequences. . . . By
> becoming fact it does not cease to be myth; that is the miracle. . . . To be
> truly Christian we must both assent to the historical fact and also receive
> the myth (fact though it has become) with the same imaginative embrace
> which we accord to all myths. The one is hardly more necessary than the
> other [emphasis in original].[36]

Similarly, as G.K. Chesterton writes, "Unless these things are appreciated
artistically they are not appreciated at all."[37] In Christ alone we may say that
myth and history meet and merge.

We might summarize: To allow a mythic or symbolic meaning to a story
does not imply that we cannot also allow for its literal or historical meaning; in
that sense, the word "myth" used by itself is not a satisfactory term for the
Redemption wrought in Christ or the accounts of his life. On the other hand, it's
also not enough to argue for the events of Redemption as *solely* historical. Not
only is Christ's life specific to human history, but also and simultaneously his
life makes up a saga or story, a story into which all of humanity is invited to
enter. These simultaneous claims *could not be made* in parallel mythic accounts
such as the story of Prometheus's "crucifixion" or Osiris's "resurrection."
Prometheus and Osiris are certainly story material, but they are not also specific

to human history; their stories are not, as the story of Christ is, fixed in history by eyewitnesses of that story. "The Gospels contain a fairy-story, or a story of a larger kind which embraces all the essence of fairy-stories," writes J.R.R. Tolkien. ". . . . But this story has entered History and the primary world; the desire and aspiration of sub-creation [mythic artistry] has been raised to the fulfillment of Creation [the realm of historical reality]."[38]

In fact, in these respects, the everyday life of every Christian is similar to the life of Christ our Forerunner. The Christian lives in history (like Christ), but also has received the eternal life of God and become part of God's eternal story of Redemption (also like Christ). We live in time and in eternity simultaneously, somewhat as Christ lives simultaneously as a historical human being and as the eternal God; in fact, the Bible teaches that in this life we *already* have been raised up into heavenly places in Christ.[39] We are to imitate Christ in all things, even in our relationship to the historical time through which we are passing—we are to live as in history and as in eternity, *at the same time.*

One more comparison may be of benefit here. The "In the beginning was the Word" of John 1:1 sounds much like the "In the beginning God created" of Genesis 1:1. However, in the case of the passage from John's Gospel, an important and qualitative change takes place, for here the Word which exists "in the beginning" is also said to become a part of chronological history, i.e., become "flesh."[40] The divine Logos becomes a human being, at a certain time, in a certain place, under certain circumstances. In answer to the query of Lévi-Strauss, "The problem is: where does mythology end and where does history start?"[41], Christianity claims that myth and history become concurrent; God's supreme action finds itself in a historical Person. So even though it's history, the Christian story is also mythic; even though it's mythic, the Christian story is also history, and should be read as such.

Many Christians seem to "panic" when they hear any discussion about the historicity of the Bible or its mythic parallels. They seem to have two thoughts on the matter: "First, if we discuss the Bible's historicity, we'll cause a lack of faith in its inspired nature and its authority; second, if we discuss mythic parallels to the Bible, we'll invite the thought that the Bible itself is just such another myth." I hope that this chapter helps to allay those thoughts. On the one hand, since God speaks to us in his Word in many different ways, it shouldn't surprise us if He uses different genres to do so; on the other hand, if God reaches out to all of humanity, it shouldn't surprise us if the mythic stories of various cultures point to Christ with various degrees of specificity, until the reality of Christ appears in history. God has spoken to us in many ways, but has now spoken to us in his Son.[42] The former myths yearn toward and reach out to the current reality.

Of course, we may disagree about all this; in particular, you may dislike the terms I use for this argument and think them misleading ("myth" or "non-literal history," for example). But at least we should lay aside the heated rhetoric about this interpretive stance being a denial of God's Word, a rejection of biblical authority, and / or disbelief of God's Truth. As believing Christians, we should strongly maintain that every part of the Bible is infallible, inerrant, inspired by God, and normative for faith and conduct. But with that belief, we don't also have to believe that every part is equally literal or historical, especially if various stories are not presented as literally historical. Doesn't that really seem more common-sensical than controversial?

Questions for Reflection:

1. Based on what you've read, give definitions satisfactory to yourself for the following terms: *non-history*; *non-literal history*; *literal history*; *myth*; *mythic patterns*.

2. One evangelical source argues that "Fiction, by its very nature, is not truth. At best, it goes beyond truth and reality."[43] On the other hand, as we've seen, C.S. Lewis holds that "fiction" may be found as part of God's inspired Word, if we read it as the Author intends us to read it. Which view do you think is more likely? With which view do you tend to agree? Why?

References

1) P.D. Feinberg, "The Inerrancy and Infallibility of the Bible." *The Evangelical Dictionary of Theology.* Edited by Walter A. Elwell. Grand Rapids, Michigan: Baker Books, 1984: 142.

2) C.S. Lewis, personal letter to Corbin Carnell, April 4, 1953. Quoted in Michael J. Christensen, *C.S. Lewis on Scripture.* Waco, Texas: Word Books, 1979: 98.

3) Francis Schaeffer, *No Final Conflict.* In *The Complete Works of Francis A. Schaeffer: Volume 2, A Christian View of the Bible as Truth.* 1st paperback edition. Westchester, Illinois: Crossway Books, 1985: 121-22.

4) Francis Schaeffer, *No Final Conflict*: 121-23.

5) Thomas Aquinas, *Quodlibetum* VII.15.3.

6) Thomas Aquinas, *Summa Theologica* I.1.10.

7) Thomas Aquinas, *Commentary on John 21*, Lecture 6.

8) *Summa Theologica* I.1.10.

9) William A. Dowd, "Inspiration." *The Catholic Encyclopedia Dictionary*. New York: The Gilmary Society, 1929: 483.

10) Charles Colson, as quoted in Hugh Hewitt, *Searching for God in America*. Dallas: Word Publishing, 1996: 17-18.

11) Isaiah 11:12.

12) Matthew 24:30.

13) Hebrews 1:1.

14) C.S. Lewis, *Miracles: A Preliminary Study*. 1st Touchstone edition. New York: Simon & Schuster, 1996: 176-77.

15) C.S. Lewis, personal letter to Corbin Carnell, April 4, 1953. Quoted in Michael J. Christensen, *C.S. Lewis on Scripture*. Waco, Texas: Word Books, 1979: 98.

16) Some of the following examples of genres are taken from Celia Brewer Marshall, *A Guide Through the Old Testament*. Louisville, Kentucky: Westminster / John Knox Press, 1989.

17) Peter Kreeft and Ronald K. Tacelli, *Handbook of Christian Apologetics*. Downers Grove, Illinois: InterVarsity Press, 1994: 207-12.

18) Michael J. Christensen, *C.S. Lewis on Scripture*. Waco, Texas: Word Books, 1979: 95.

19) C.S. Lewis, "The World's Last Night." From *The World's Last Night and Other Essays*. 6th printing. San Diego: Harvest / HBJ Publishing, 1973: 98-99.

20) See, for example, John 1:14, 20:30, 21:24, and 1 John 1:1-3.

21) Luke 1:1-4.

22) 1 Cor. 15:6.

23) Mark 14:51-52.

24) Acts 16:10.

25) Matthew 20:29-34; Mark 10:46-52.

26) C.L. Blomberg, "Historical Reliability of the Gospels." *The IVP Dictionary of the New Testament*. Edited by Daniel G. Reid. Downers Grove, Illinois: InterVarsity Press, 2004: 457.

27) Peter Kreeft, *Between Heaven and Hell*. Downers Grove, Illinois: InterVarsity Press, 1982: 75.

28) 1 Cor. 1:23.

29) Claude Lévi-Strauss, *Myth and Meaning.* New York: Schocken Books, 1979: 38.

30) Most of the material of this section is taken from Craig Payne, *Where Myth and History Meet: A Christian Response to Myth.* Lanham, Maryland: University Press of America, 2001.

31) Eric Voegelin, *Conversations with Eric Voegelin.* Edited by R. Eric O'Connor. Montreal: Thomas More Institute, 1980: 2.

32) Peter Kreeft and Ronald K. Tacelli, *Handbook of Christian Apologetics*: 153-54.

33) Ernest F. Scott, "The New Testament and Criticism." *The Abingdon Bible Commentary.* New York: Abingdon Press, 1929: 886-87.

34) C.S. Lewis, as quoted in Douglas Gilbert and Clyde S. Kilby, *C.S. Lewis: Images of His World.* Grand Rapids, Michigan: Eerdmans, 1973: 21.

35) C.S. Lewis, *Surprised by Joy.* New York: Harcourt Brace Jovanovich, 1955: 236.

36) C.S. Lewis, "Myth Became Fact." *God in the Dock: Essays on Theology and Ethics.* Edited by Walter Hooper. Grand Rapids, Michigan: Eerdmans Publishing Co., 1970: 66-67.

37) G.K. Chesterton, *The Everlasting Man.* In *The Collected Works of G.K. Chesterton, Volume II.* Edited by George J. Marlin, Richard P. Rabatin, and John L. Swan. San Francisco: Ignatius Press, 1986: 233.

38) J.R.R. Tolkien, "On Fairy-Stories." *Tree and Leaf.* London: George Allen & Unwin Ltd., 1964: 71-72.

39) Ephesians 2:4-6.

40) John 1:14.

41) Claude Lévi-Strauss, *Myth and Meaning*: 38.

42) Hebrews 1:1-2.

43) Biblical Discernment Ministries, "Book Review: The *Left Behind* Series." March 2004. rapidnet.com.

Chapter 5: What Is a Human?

"All the light in us is turned to darkness, as the Scripture teaches us. . . . We believe that by the disobedience of Adam original sin has been spread through the whole human race. It is a corruption of all nature—an inherited depravity which even infects small infants in their mother's womb, and the root which produces in man every sort of sin. [This sin] constantly boils forth as though from a contaminated spring. . . . [T]he awareness of this corruption might often make believers groan as they long to be set free from the 'body of this death.'"—Guido de Bräs, The Belgic Confession.

I'm OK, You're OK—book title.

"What a chimera, then, is man! What a novelty! What a monster, what a chaos, what a contradiction, what a prodigy! Judge of all things, feeble worm of the earth, depository of truth, a sink of uncertainty and error, the glory and the shame of the universe."—Blaise Pascal.

Our Unnatural Nature

Many centuries before J.R.R. Tolkien's *Lord of the Rings*, with its One Ring of Power that grants invisibility to those who use it but ultimately corrupts them, the story of the Ring of Gyges was known. In Book II of *The Republic*, Plato's elder brother Glaucon tells the story to Socrates as follows: Gyges was a humble shepherd in the service of a king. "One day there was a great storm, and the ground where his flock was feeding was rent by an earthquake."[1] Entering the chasm created by the earthquake, Gyges finds a huge body, naked except for a ring which Gyges takes.

Later, at a meeting of the King's shepherds, Gyges discovers the ring's remarkable property: When he twists it on his finger he becomes invisible, and when he twists it back, he reappears. "After this discovery he contrived to be one of the messengers sent to the court. There he seduced the Queen, and with her help murdered the King and seized the throne."

Here's an interesting question, one I often pose to students: Let's suppose you yourself had something like the Ring of Gyges. What do you suppose would happen to you morally? "Would you use this ring of invisibility to do all the good things you've always wanted to do, but haven't done for fear of the publicity?" I ask them. "Would you go around putting money into poor people's pockets? Would you invisibly trim hedges in the summer and scrape icy windshields in the winter? Would you use this ring only because you always have desired to help others, but wished to do so anonymously?" When I ask these questions, the response from students is always the same: They break into uneasy laughter as they recognize that perhaps the good behaviors they exhibit don't really come from an innately good human nature. Perhaps if we didn't have centuries of biblical moral training, or the habitual reinforcement of natural conscience, or even just the fear of social exposure—if, say, we had the power of invisibility—perhaps we wouldn't be the good people we reassuringly tell ourselves we are. "Hence, how much soever men may disguise their impurity," as one Christian writer states, "some are restrained only by shame, others by a fear of the laws, from breaking out into many kinds of wickedness."[2]

Glaucon himself has no doubts on the matter:

> Now suppose there were two such magic rings, and one were given to the just man, the other to the unjust. No one, it is commonly believed, would have such iron strength of mind as to stand fast in doing right or keep his hands off other men's goods, when he could go to the marketplace and fearlessly help himself to anything he wanted, enter houses and sleep with any woman he chose, set prisoners free and kill men at his pleasure, and in a word go about among men with the powers of a god. He would behave no better than the other; both would take the same course. Surely this would be strong proof that men do right only under compulsion; no individual thinks of it as good for him personally, since he does wrong whenever he finds he has the power.[3]

Socrates gives a partial argument against this view, maintaining that to do good actually *is* better for every individual than to do wrong, even if the good is unrecognized by society. Much later, he brings up Glaucon's example again: "We have found that, apart from all such consequences, justice is the best thing for the soul, which should do what is right, whether or not it possess the ring of Gyges."[4] However, we might agree with Socrates' view of justice and the soul, what humans *should* do, while still also agreeing with Glaucon's description of what humans in actual practice *would* do given Gyges' ring.

Really, how long would it take for a ring of invisibility to corrupt our moral behavior? And if our moral behavior can be so readily corrupted, what does that tell us about our true moral *nature*? Socrates himself thought that humans are innately good and only fall into wrongdoing through ignorance; however, it may be true that, as one writer asserts, "Socrates had his own *daemon* [voice of conscience], but he did not know the Demon."[5] Do we unduly flatter ourselves regarding our true innermost tendencies? When Samuel Johnson was touring Scotland with Boswell, a certain Lady Macleod asked him whether or not he thought humans were naturally and innately good. "No, madam," came Johnson's rapidfire reply, "no more than a wolf!" Boswell remonstrated by asking, "Nor no woman, sir?" but again Johnson replied, "No, sir."[6] Did Johnson's wide experience of humanity cause his certainty in this matter?

On the other hand, human history is also full of goodness, replete with examples of truly altruistic behavior. There actually *have* lived people who have sacrificed their lives anonymously for the good of others. Even though we see fewer instances of it than we would prefer, humans really do seem to possess this innate nobility and virtue of character, the "voice of conscience" mentioned earlier. As the Bible puts it, natural humans "having not the law" still "show the work of the law written in their hearts."[7] We seem to have other innermost tendencies besides the wrongful.

Of course, the Bible itself reveals the source of this "split personality" in humanity. It teaches that humans are *Imago Dei*, both males and females created in the image of God Himself.[8] But it also teaches that humans have fallen away from this image, that Original Sin has altered and twisted this image into something defiled and sinful.[9] "What a horrible teaching!" an atheist friend of mine used to exclaim to me, shaking her head in dismay. "It corrupts the beauty and innocence of the whole world." However, when we look at it another way, it is truly a *wonderful* teaching. It tells me there is a *reason* for this nature of mine—it tells me there is a reason I can always see the good I desire to do, but can never quite do it. It explains why I can always imagine the godlike person I desire to be but never quite seem to be able to become. It tells me that my amazing and awe-inspiring dreams, aspirations, and divine ideals are there for a reason (my Original Creation in God's image), but that my actual performance, my continual falling short, my sinfulness and carnality, also have an explanation (the Original Sin in us all, primarily manifested in my weak, easily tempted will).

Without the doctrine of Original Sin to help us understand ourselves, it would seem we humans would live in constant hopeless despair at our divided condition, our seemingly "unnatural nature." We would cry out with Paul, "For the good that I would I do not, but the evil which I would not, that I do. . . . O wretched man that I am! Who shall deliver me?" However, we know that Paul doesn't stop there, but continues: "I thank God through Jesus Christ our Lord."[10] The answer to the question "Who shall deliver us?" is clearly implied: God will, in Christ.

In other words, thank God for the knowledge and hope that the doctrine of Original Sin provides—the knowledge that there is a reason for our condition, and the hope that *we really can become a new creation*, the hope Christians see fulfilled in Christ and our Redemption. By God's grace, should we accept it, we are not permanently "stuck" in our fallen selves, with no explanation as to how we got there.

However, this soberly realistic doctrine pointing forward to God's salvation in Christ also has caused division within Christ's Body. Intense theological battles have erupted over the question, believe it or not, "Exactly how fallen *are* we?" What is the extent of Original Sin? Further, numerous subsidiary questions sprawl out from this central one: What does Christ's redemptive work accomplish for us? In other words, exactly what does the Crucifixion do, or what is *required* for it to do? Do we actually have free will to accept God's offer of salvation? Or is our will also so fallen that it is enslaved, and so we cannot receive salvation on our own but require God's spiritual help? If the latter is correct, why doesn't God just help everyone's will to receive salvation? How far does the corruption from the Fall permeate throughout the goodness of God's creation? Can humans come to know some things about God and redemption through the use of their natural reason? Or is reason itself also fallen and corrupted?

Often we refer to the framework within which these questions and others arise as the teaching of "Total Depravity." The outlines of this teaching may be found in Augustine and Luther, but today are indissolubly linked to the name of John Calvin and the entire Christian system of thought known as Calvinism. In fact, Total Depravity is the first of the famous "Five Points" of Calvinism:

- Total depravity.

- Unconditional election.

- Limited atonement.

- Irresistible grace.

- Perseverance of the saints, better known as the "Once saved, always saved" teaching. (Taken together, these five points are referred to as TULIP for short.)

We might understand the problem raised by the idea of Total Depravity better by putting it this way: Is the Original Sin an "ontic" fall, through which every single feature of humanity is corrupted and untrustworthy, including its natural reason and virtue? Or is the Original Sin of humanity a "moral" fall, something more like a deprivation of our original righteousness, a deprivation through which all humans now possess the innate tendency to make wrongful decisions and thus commit sin? In other words, do all humans since the Fall exist in a state of "Total Depravity" or do they not?

In this chapter, I certainly do not intend to try to resolve this battle or answer this question. However, I would like to argue for this conclusion: Both Scripture and philosophical tradition can be brought to bear to support the arguments both in favor of and against the idea of Total Depravity; because of this, the many charges of "heresy" flung back and forth due to this issue are both uncharitable and *biblically unwarranted.* Therefore, the exact nature of humanity's fallenness should not be an issue in which faithful, biblical Christians are required to accept one side or the other.

Stated simply: The Total Depravity of the human person is a doctrine believers don't have to believe.

Questions for Reflection:

1. I hope that you were considering yourself as you read the story of the Ring of Gyges. What do you think? Would possession of this ring corrupt your moral behavior or not? Let's shift location from Greece to Middle-Earth in order to ask this question: If you had the ring, would you gradually change from Smeagol to Gollum?

2. I referred to the "hope" that the "wonderful" doctrine of Original Sin provides us. Have you ever thought of it this way? Do you agree or disagree? If you could, would you remove the story of the Fall from Christian teaching? Why or why not?

3. Have you ever heard the term "Total Depravity" before reading this? How would you define it? Have you ever heard of "Calvinism"? What have you heard?

Total Depravity: Arguments in Favor

Calvinist advocates of the Total Depravity doctrine seem to have in mind a good motivation for holding this view. Of course, they believe it is taught by the Bible, but they also think of it as the only way to preserve completely God's sovereignty and almighty nature. If humans have free will, they argue, or if humans have retained some trustworthy natural powers by which they might attain some knowledge of God, doesn't that entail that a measure of our salvation is by our own "works" rather than by God's grace? If humans "choose" to accept salvation, doesn't that mean their salvation results at least partially from their own efforts (their choice) rather than their salvation being entirely of God's irresistible grace and mercy? Isn't it a denial of God's sovereignty to say that humans can "choose" to be saved?

Here's how one Calvinist author states the issue:

> Because of the Fall, man is unable of himself to savingly believe the gospel. The sinner is dead, blind, and deaf to the things of God; his heart is deceitful and desperately corrupt. His will is not free; it is in bondage to his evil nature; therefore, he will not—indeed he cannot—choose good over evil in the spiritual realm.[11]

Calvin himself is the prime fountainhead for this line of thought. "There is no salvation for man, save in the mercy of God, because in himself he is desperate and undone," he writes.[12] ". . . . The soul . . . not only labors under vice, but is altogether devoid of good." Even our rational faculties have been radically vitiated and stripped of their native goodness, so that the natural knowledge of God gained through reason (as found in Aquinas's philosophy, for example) is seen as impossible either to trust or even to receive: "The human mind receives a humbling blow when all the thoughts which proceed from it are derided as foolish, frivolous, perverse, and insane."[13] According to Calvin, the definition of "flesh" as used in the New Testament includes all human natural properties, everything we have "from nature," and these properties are thus worthless when it comes to the knowledge of God:

> The intellect and will of man are so corrupted, that no integrity, no knowledge or fear of God, can now be found in him. . . . Is it true that the flesh is so perverse, that it is perpetually striving with all its might against God? That it cannot accord with the righteousness of the divine law? That, in short, it can beget nothing but the materials of death? Grant that there is nothing in human nature but flesh, and then extract something good out of it if you can. . . . Everything . . . which we have from nature is flesh.[14]

Following Calvin's thinking, his contemporary Guido de Brás in 1561 produced a document which came to be known as the "Belgic Confession." In the early 1600s all officebearers in the Calvinist Reformed churches were required to accept this Confession, and it still stands today as a more or less typical statement of Reformed doctrine. Article 14 of the Belgic Confession, "The Creation and Fall of Man," reads in part, "All the light in us is turned to darkness, as the Scripture teaches us. . . . Therefore we reject everything taught to the contrary concerning man's free will, since man is nothing but the slave of sin and cannot do a thing unless it is 'given to him from heaven' [John 3:27]." Article 15, "The Doctrine of Original Sin," continues:

> We believe that by the disobedience of Adam original sin has been spread through the whole human race. It is a corruption of all nature—an inherited depravity which even infects small infants in their mother's womb, and the root which produces in man every sort of sin. [This sin] constantly boils forth as though from a contaminated spring. . . . [T]he awareness of this corruption might often make believers groan as they long to be set free from the 'body of this death' [Romans 7:24].[15]

As befitting the beliefs of its Protestant proponents, the doctrine of Total Depravity is not supported, as we can see, by philosophical or confessional arguments alone. Along with their arguments against human free will and the natural powers of human reason, Calvinist authors also point to many scriptural passages which seem to support the teaching of Total Depravity. In the relevant sections of his *Institutes*, Calvin points to Paul's words in the epistle to the Romans: "There is none righteous, no, not one: There is none that understandeth, there is none that seeketh after God. They are all gone out of the way, they are together become unprofitable; there is none that doeth good, no, not one."[16] Other commonly cited passages include the following:

Supporting the total lack of human goodness:

- The heart is deceitful above all things, and desperately wicked: who can know it?[17]
- And you hath He quickened, who were dead in trespasses and sins. . . . [W]e all had our conversation in times past in the lusts of our flesh, fulfilling the desires of the flesh and of the mind; and were by nature the children of wrath, even as others.[18]
- Destruction and misery are in their ways: and the way of peace have they not known: There is no fear of God before their eyes.[19]

Supporting the lack of human free will:

- All that the Father giveth me shall come to me. . . . No man can come to me, except the Father which hath sent me draw him: and I will raise him up at the last day.[20]
- . . . [T]hat the purpose of God according to election might stand, not of works, but of Him that calleth, it was said unto her, The elder shall serve the younger. . . . For He saith to Moses, I will have mercy on whom I will have mercy, and I will have compassion on whom I will have compassion. So then it is not of him that willeth, nor of him that runneth, but of God that sheweth mercy. . . . Therefore hath He mercy on whom He will have mercy, and whom He will he hardeneth. Thou wilt say then unto me, Why doth He yet find fault? For who hath resisted his will? Nay but, O man, who art thou that repliest against God? Shall the thing formed say to him that formed it, Why hast thou made me thus? Hath not the potter power over the clay, of the same lump to make one vessel unto honor, and another unto dishonor?[21]

So we see that both Scriptural and philosophical argumentation can be brought to bear to support the idea of Total Depravity. As historian Erik von Kuehnelt-Leddihn summarizes:

[According to Calvinism] man is a wretched creature totally crippled by Original Sin . . . God's grace alone can save him. . . . We are left with an enfeebled will, a darkened understanding, and a strong inclination to evil; the belief that man is good and becomes bad only in desperation is utter nonsense. . . . One must face the fact that man is a sinner, that he is weak and inclined to be wicked. No scientific or philosophical preparation is

needed to recognize this sad truth: all we need do is look into our own lives
and into our own souls to realize that we have at least the potentiality for
great evil.[22]

Questions for Reflection:

1.   Often Calvinist teaching is described as "harsh." Do you think it
     is? Does its supposed harshness have anything to do with
     whether or not Calvinism is accurate?

2.   Earlier I asked the questions, "Is our will also so fallen that it is
     enslaved, and so we cannot receive salvation on our own but
     require God's spiritual help? If the latter is correct, why doesn't
     God just help everyone to will to receive salvation?" One
     common response to these questions is that since all of us have
     sinned, we all *deserve* damnation. Therefore, God is perfectly
     justified to allow some to go to Hell even while He graciously
     moves the wills of others to accept Him and thus be saved. We
     shouldn't question why He elects some for salvation and others
     not. If He does not so elect some, but allows them to continue
     on in their way to eternal punishment, that is his right and their
     due.
          What do you think of this argument?

3.   Do you think of your will as being free? (A "free" will requires
     that our choices not be coerced or determined by God or any
     other force to such a degree that we could not choose otherwise
     than we do.) Do you think of your choice to accept Christ as
     being free?

4.   Do you think of your rationality as being trustworthy? Why or
     why not?

Total Depravity: Arguments Against

Of course, not all Christians accept the doctrine of the Total Depravity of
the human person. "The Bible clearly teaches the sin nature and evil ways of
mankind," according to one Protestant source. "This is the case with every
person and is fully supported by Scripture, but Scripture certainly does not teach
a state of Total Depravity or Total Inability." The idea of Total Depravity is later
described by the same author as an "exaggeration" of the Scriptural descriptions
of humanity.[23] Moreover, within evangelical Protestantism the teaching of
"Arminianism" (from Reformation thinker James Arminius) is at least as
popular as Calvinism; according to the Arminian system of thought, the Fall of

humanity can be thought of as a "deprivation" of the original state of righteousness, rather than as an actual metaphysical quality of evil or depravity.[24]

Eastern Orthodox Christians also have a much different understanding of the nature of the Fall and the human condition, rejecting the powerful influence of Augustine within the Roman Catholic Church:

> In the Byzantine world, where Augustinian thought exercised practically no influence, the significance of the sin of Adam and of its consequences for mankind was understood along quite different lines. . . . [N]either original sin nor salvation can be realized in an individual's life without involving his personal and free responsibility. . . . There is indeed a consensus in Greek patristic and Byzantine traditions in identifying the inheritance of the Fall as an inheritance essentially of mortality rather than of sinfulness.[25]

Furthermore, even within the Roman Catholic world, Augustine's views often are interpreted in a different sense than the way Calvin interpreted them during the Reformation period. In fact, in his early thought, Augustine himself was in agreement with the Eastern tradition, interpreting Adam's punishment as "inherited mortality" rather than as "inherited guilt"; he did not introduce the term "Original Sin" (*peccatum originale*) until A.D. 396.[26] Augustine developed and amplified this view considerably in later works; still, the debate continues in contemporary scholarship over "the status and dynamics of Augustine's position on inherited sin."[27]

By way of example of this debate, let's consider this statement from Augustine: "The deed is the evil thing, not the thing of which the sinner makes an evil use. Evil is making a bad use of a good thing."[28] For instance, your hands can be used to caress a child's head or build a shelter for the needy. However, they can also be used to abuse a child or wield a weapon in murder. In other words, the hands themselves are not inherently evil, nor are they naturally corrupted. They are not any more prone to the bad action as to the good; it all depends on the good or evil will of the possessor of the hands. So it is with the other natural goods of creation: sex, for instance, is a natural good, but can be easily misused, perhaps even more easily (because it goes nearer to the heart of our nature) than other natural goods. As a natural good, food can be used to rescue people from starvation or used to help provide a pleasurable evening with friends, but it also can be used to satiate gluttonous tendencies or gain illegitimate control over other humans. Virtually all of the good things of God's creation can be misused in evil ways, while the things themselves remain good.

Now what about human reason? And what about freedom of the will? Here are two crucial ways opponents of the idea of Total Depravity differ from those proposing it: Opponents tend to think of human rationality and freedom as natural goods, like human hands or lungs or sexuality. Of course, because they are so intimately manifestations of who we are in our fallenness, the human cognitive and volitional faculties are highly susceptible to evil uses—but even so, those evil uses do not negate the inherent good and natural trustworthiness of these faculties. The laws of logic are structurally valid and can be used by our reason to discover valid and trustworthy truths concerning God and his universe, even though we humans too often use our logical resources to plan and carry out (and then defend our participation in) evil or at least questionable actions. Likewise the fact of a free will is a good, though we may use our freedom to make evil choices.

In his *Fundamentals of Catholic Dogma*, Ludwig Ott states this view of the natural goods remaining within humanity as the standard Roman Catholic view:

> The wounding of nature must not be conceived, with the Reformers [he is writing specifically of Calvin and Luther] and the Jansenists, as the complete corruption of human nature. In the condition of Original Sin, man possesses the ability of knowing natural religious truths and of performing natural morally good actions. . . . [For example:] Man, with his natural power of cognition, can with certainty know the existence of God. The Council of Trent teaches that free will was not lost or extinguished by the fall of Adam.[29]

Of course, this directly flies against the Calvinist position that the will is now inherently bound in sin's fetters and that human rationality is corrupt, useless, and even frivolous for all helpful theological purposes. However, this is not just an anti-Protestant "Catholic" position; in fact, it is remarkably similar to that stated by evangelical Ronald B. Mayers, a professor at Grand Rapids Baptist College and Seminary. In his work *Both / And: A Balanced Apologetic*, Mayers argues for the following, which sounds much like Ott's "standard" Roman Catholic statement:

> The Fall of man does not destroy man's rational powers. The Bible holds man responsible for the light that he has (John 1:4-9; Romans 1:20). If man's rational abilities were destroyed at the Fall, there would be no intelligible argument possible to the unbeliever. All preaching, especially evangelistic preaching, presumes that unsaved man can intellectually comprehend the cognitive content and moral obligation of the gospel. The Bible is eliminated if the revelation therein cannot be intelligibly appropriated. The divine image in man was effaced and misdirected, but not destroyed.[30]

Therefore, what we have seen is that throughout Christianity, whether of the Protestant, Eastern Orthodox, or Roman Catholic varieties, the view of the human as bound by Total Depravity is certainly anything but universal. We seem to have good reason to ask the question: Is it a view that is important enough to divide us?

As with the defenders of the doctrine of Total Depravity, opponents can point both to philosophical and to scriptural supports for their position. For an example of the philosophical support, we might look to Thomas Aquinas, who thinks of our creation "in God's image" as meaning our intellectual likeness to God. The word "intellectual" in the Thomist sense means more than what we typically mean by it; it means that within humans which is both immaterial and superior to the material.

> Moreover, the higher a thing is in the scale of being, the closer it draws to likeness with God. Thus we observe that some things (e.g., those pertaining to the lowest degree, such as lifeless beings) share in the divine likeness with respect to existence only; others, however (such as plants), share in the divine likeness with respect to existence and life; and yet others (such as animals) share in the divine likeness with respect to sense perception. But the highest degree—and that which makes us most like to God—is conferred by the intellect.
>
> Consequently, the most excellent creatures are intellectual [Thomas means humans, as will be seen in the following sentence]. Indeed, they are said to be fashioned in God's image for the very reason that among all creatures they approach most closely to likeness with God.[31]

Again, it is the use of the thing and not the thing itself which is evil; therefore, the intellectual faculties of humanity are not evil. They may even be used in ways of "natural" morality and in order to apprehend "natural" theological truths. For an example of the use of the intellect to recognize natural *moral* truths, we may point to the continuing widespread opposition to the idea of "gay marriage." In elections held in eleven American states in 2004, legalization of "gay marriage" lost by wide margins in all eleven states; this shows that people in general recognize that the issue is not a "religious question," as it is insistently proclaimed to be by news media, but is an issue of natural morality, the knowledge of which is accessible to all. For an example of the use of the intellect to recognize natural *theological* truths, we may point to the widespread knowledge of God's existence and character in surprisingly similar particulars throughout the world.

Aquinas continues his argument for the intellectual likeness to God in humans with a defense of human free will. "This fact [of intellectual likeness to God] shows that such beings have freedom of choice." Humans do not act apart from judgment, as for example a moving river does. Neither do they act solely on impulse, as lower animals do:

> For the intellect perceives the end, the means leading to the end, and the bearing of one on the other. Hence the intellect can be the cause of its own judgment, whereby it desires a good and performs an action for the sake of an end.
>
> But what is a cause unto itself is precisely what we call free. Accordingly, the intellect desires and acts in virtue of a free judgment, which is the same as having freedom of choice.[32]

For the intellect to be "the cause of its own judgment" and "a cause unto itself" does not mean it can act as an "Unmoved Mover" or "Uncaused Cause," prerogatives and titles belonging only to God. Just as events in nature proceed "naturally" by nature's laws because of the action of God in nature, so also the free human will proceeds naturally (that is to say, *freely*) because of the action of God in the will. God is the primary efficient cause and the human agent the secondary efficient cause of any free action; in other words, human freedom exists because of God and free human actions exist because of the human agent. In this sense only is the human intellect "the cause of its own judgment" and thus the mover of the will; still, this secondary sense is quite enough for genuine human freedom to exist. After all, when we enter a restaurant, we don't sit patiently, waiting to see what will be ordered by us. No, we choose and we order. The freedom comes from God alone; the choice comes from us.

This is actually the relatively simple answer to the common objection that humans cannot be free because God infallibly predetermines all things, and his knowledge and will cannot be resisted. "After all," we sometimes hear, "God already knows exactly what I'm going to do, right?" One can accept this as perfectly true, and yet also accept that the human will proceeds freely *because of* God's action in the will. Aquinas makes this same point in the *Summa Theologica*: "[Now all things happen] either by necessity or by contingency. Therefore whatever divine providence ordains to happen infallibly and of necessity happens infallibly and of necessity; and that happens from contingency, which the plan of divine providence conceives to happen from contingency."[33] Humans have free will precisely *because* God's knowledge and will cannot be resisted. He has infallibly predetermined that humans have free will and can make contingent choices, and so we do and can. If you are trying to figure out how God can allow human freedom without imposing on it the character of necessity, given his absolute and infallible knowledge of our choices—well, He is all-powerful, too. As Samuel Johnson puts it, in his typically pungent style, "Sir, we *know* our will is free, and there's an end on't."

So we see that human freedom, contrary to the Calvinist view, is not a denial of God's sovereignty; in fact, it is actually a *result* of God's sovereign action. We have no choice but to accept our freedom. Faith is not a "work," but a reception, and our free choices a miraculous part of God's irresistible providence.

Along with the philosophical arguments, opponents of Total Depravity also find support from the Bible itself. Here are a few sample scriptures:

Supporting the natural theological capabilities of the human intellect:

- Come now, and let us reason together, saith the Lord.[34]
- The heavens declare the glory of God; and the firmament sheweth his handiwork. Day unto day uttereth speech, and night unto night sheweth knowledge. There is no speech nor language, where their voice is not heard. [Or, "Although they have no speech or language and their voice is not heard . . ."] Their line is

gone out through all the earth, and their words to the end of the world. [This passage and the next few imply a "natural" revelation, accessible to all humans.][35]

- He [God] left not himself without witness, in that He did good, and gave us rain from heaven, and fruitful seasons, filling our hearts with food and gladness.[36]
- Doth not even nature itself teach you . . .?[37]
- [Jesus is] the true Light, which lighteth every man that cometh into the world. [This is often interpreted as referring to the *lumen naturale*, a natural light by which all humans may follow Christ's teachings at least to an extent without consciously recognizing Who it is they are following.][38]
- Of a truth I perceive that God is no respecter of persons: But in every nation he that feareth Him, and worketh righteousness, is accepted with Him.[39]
- Because that which may be known of God is manifest in them; for God hath shewed it unto them. For the invisible things of Him from the creation of the world are clearly seen, being understood by the things that are made, even his eternal power and Godhead; so that they are without excuse.[40]

Supporting human free will:

- For whosoever shall call upon the name of the Lord shall be saved. [This scripture and especially the next would seem senseless if the acceptance of salvation were not a free choice.][41]
- I have set before you life and death, blessing and cursing: therefore choose life, that both thou and thy seed may live.[42]
- They hated knowledge, and did not choose the fear of the Lord. Therefore shall they eat of the fruit of their own way, and be filled with their own devices.[43]
- [R]efuse the evil, and choose the good.[44]
- When the wicked man turneth away from his wickedness . . . he shall save his soul alive. Because he considereth, and turneth away from all his transgressions that he hath committed, he shall surely live, he shall not die. . . . For I have no pleasure in the death of him that dieth, saith the Lord God: wherefore turn yourselves, and live ye.[45]
- Choose you this day whom ye will serve . . . but as for me and my house, we will serve the Lord.[46]

It is probably fairly obvious by now that I don't agree with the Total Depravity teaching regarding our human condition before God. Along with multitudes of other Christians, I think Original Sin may be understood as a "moral" fall, not necessarily an "ontic" fall. However, whether I do or do not agree with this is not important. The main point is that both philosophical argumentation and Scripture can be used to support both sides of this debate; therefore, it is not required of believers that they hold one specific view or the other on Total Depravity. This is also true regarding this doctrine's spin-off issues:

- The extent of our Redemption through Christ's Crucifixion and Resurrection.
- The nature of God's sovereignty.
- Whether or not we have free will to accept God's offer of salvation.
- The extent of our will's bondage.
- The nature and origin of our faith in God.
- The question of God's salvific election.
- The question of whether or not we are "once saved, always saved."
- The trustworthiness of our natural reason.
- The extent of our natural knowledge of God.
- And so on.

All of these are important issues. However, they are issues over which equally committed and biblical Christians may differ. They should not divide us.

Questions for Reflection:

1. In some Protestant circles, the question of whether one is a Calvinist or Arminian is a hot topic. After having read about both Calvin and Arminius (admittedly, very little is to be found in this chapter about either one), toward which do you lean? Why? Do you have any desire to learn more about either?

2. I quoted Augustine: "The deed is the evil thing, not the thing of which the sinner makes an evil use. Evil is making a bad use of a good thing." In the Christian view, all things are naturally good, having been created by an all-good Lord. However, we often hear people, even Christians, say something like, "We need to have evil existing in the world; otherwise, we'd have no way to appreciate the good." What do you think of this statement? Do you think Adam and Eve appreciated God's goodness before the Fall? If so, is the statement misleading? If so, how would you correct those people who say it?

3. Do you think humans can know moral truths and act upon them apart from the Christian faith? Do you think people can know God's existence apart from the Christian faith? If your answer is "Yes" to these questions, how does this "natural" revelation relate to the Christian revelation? If your answer is "No" to these questions, do you think God has any dealings at all with any humans in any way outside of the Christian revelation?

4. I listed several biblical verses both in favor of the teachings surrounding Total Depravity and against those teachings. Which scriptural selections did you find more convincing? Why?

Dante's Vision and Our Destiny

When human nature is viewed in the two-fold way we've been discussing—as (1) fallen, mortal, and morally degraded, and yet (2) created in God's image, possessing possibilities of freedom and non-material intellect almost divine in scope—our understanding of Christ Himself is also expanded. Christians no longer live in either a "God-centered" or a "man-centered" universe; rather, we now live in a "Christ-centered" universe. The Incarnation makes the universe of the New Creation[47] both God-centered *and*, in the Person of Christ the God-man, man-centered—for Christ is one of us, and will be so throughout eternity. When man makes himself the center of his universe, he commits a horrendous and devilish sin. But when God Himself moves man to his new status of being seated together with Christ in heavenly places, He brings about a stupendous and awe-inspiring Redemption: "But God, who is rich in mercy, for his great love wherewith He loved us, even when we were dead in sins, hath quickened us together with Christ (by grace ye are saved), and hath raised us up together and made us sit together in heavenly places in Christ."[48]

Of course, we can in no way say that man "deserved" this in himself. The continual chatter about the "dignity" of humanity can quickly become depresssing if not tempered with a realistic assessment of our actual condition. However, the word of grace we have before us is that God, in his kindness and mercy, redeemed us anyway. The Incarnation does not necessarily imply a special virtue or excellence; in fact, as C.S. Lewis writes:

> It implies just the reverse: a particular demerit and depravity. No creature that deserved Redemption would need to be redeemed. They that are whole need not the physician. Christ died for men precisely because men are *not* worth dying for; to make them worth it.[49]

But what is done is done, and God is now at work in us: "We are his workmanship, created in Christ Jesus unto good works."[50] He desires our reconciliation with Himself, for the sake of his own love and not our worthiness, badly enough to take upon Himself the limitations of suffering and circumscribed humanity. He reaches out through Christ to mend us, so that we might share his glory as a mirror shares the glory of the reality before it, or (better and more scriptural) as a child shares the glory of the parent. In this point of view, God is the original "humanist"—and if these thoughts bring about a certain "self-esteem," it is only because of the previous work of God's esteem. The Church, blessed thought, has become "accepted in the Beloved."[51]

One of the greatest literary works to present this truth, perhaps the greatest outside of the inspired canon itself, is the epic fourteenth-century poem *The Divine Comedy*, by Dante Alighieri. The poem follows Dante's progression as he descends into hell in the *Inferno*, climbs Mount Purgatory in the *Purgatorio*, and passes through the heavenlies in order finally to gain the beatific vision of God in the *Paradiso*, in the center of the White Rose formed by the spiritual bodies of the redeemed saints. The poem is an extraordinarily intricate picture of the progress of the human soul in redemption, and—more to our point—a brilliant fusion of the doctrines of the inherently fallen nature of man and of his creation in God's image.

This picture of the human soul, for instance, can be seen in the *Purgatorio*. As Dante climbs up the side of Mount Purgatory toward heaven and the vision of God, he is met by a succession of figures drawn variously from mythology, history, his own time, and the Bible; these figures represent vices, against which Dante is warned, and their parallel virtues, which he is encouraged to emulate. These alternating examples of vice and virtue are sometimes translated in metaphorical form as Dante's "curbs" and "goads," or even his "bridle" and "spurs." Thus, in the pathway toward eternal bliss, he sees both the good and evil to which humans in the way of salvation are prone, or of which they are capable. He sees not only the examples of humanity which are used as curbs or bridles to his baser passions, but also those examples which are used as goads or spurs for his virtuous desires and aspirations.

The point is that in Dante's view of human nature, we need not only the bridle, but also the spur; not only the restraints placed upon our fallen nature, but also the encouragement offered to the sacred spark lying within us as the image and glory and crowning creation of God. We cannot live by the letter, which exists to point out our sinfulness; we must live by the Spirit, which simultaneously convicts us of sin *and* allows us to partake of the very character of God in Christ (in Christ, of course, as the plan of God for us is summarized and brought to a head in Him, unique in being fully God and fully human). Through Him we become "partakers of the divine nature."[52]

As he reaches the summit of the *Paradiso*, Dante sees humanity in its finest flower, so to speak, seated in the image of the White Rose, the petals of which swirl inward to a brilliant central Light. Here the saints contemplate the beatific vision of God at the rational level, according to Aristotle and Aquinas the highest level of the soul's development. Here Beatrice, Dante's beloved inspiration and guide, returns to her eternal joy.

And in the very center of the Rose Dante finally sees the vision of God. After his arduous journeys through "the three realms of the spirit," he is rewarded by looking upon God Himself. And in that vision, in the midst of the three concentric circles of pure radiance, he sees—a human face.

Of course, this is Christ, the God-man, God the Son, God Incarnate. But Dante never *names* this face, never tells us who this Human might be. Could it be Christ appearing as God united to humanity—could it be a glimpse of you and me "in the Beloved," God's mended image finally returned to its Source, finally sharing that divine life and light which God has desired to share with us all along?

Humans are not completely spirit, as is God. We are incomplete, or incompletely human, without our natural minds and bodies. Yet we have the promise that God will one day bring about the Redemption of the totality of us, and that we will be one in Him even as He is Three and yet One. How will this be accomplished? Only in Christ, in Whom we even now are seated spiritually as we accept his finished work on our behalf. In Christ—in Him—in the Beloved—these are phrases which resound over and over again throughout the Epistles to the Church. Perhaps they are phrases we should take more seriously than we often do.

So we see that we can respond both in positive and in negative terms to the question, "What, then, is a human?" Both the recognition of our innate potential and our fallen nature are necessary for health and wholeness in personality and in Christian dialogue. As professor and essayist Robert B. Heilman has written, these contradictory responses come about because "the central disparateness is that of human nature itself." He goes on:

> Everyman is both saint and devil; true, in this man or at this time, one may speak louder than the other; but we dare not forget that both are there. In cynical moods we forget the saint; in utopian moods, the devil.

Dr. Heilman points out that we commonly accept this disparateness in everyday life:

> We accept the romantic and the realistic in man, the rational and the irrational, the necessity of work as well as of leisure; we know that he seeks freedom but likewise deeply craves bounds and bonds, that he seeks the required as well as the chosen. And we better know that he is both conservative and liberal, that being both is indispensable, and that both contain the seeds of both vice and virtue.[53]

Which provides the segue into our next chapter.

Questions for Reflection:

1. I have heard Christians arguing that humanism presents a "man-centered" universe, while Christianity presents a "God-centered"

universe. In this part of the chapter, I've tried to convey that both of these are comprehended in a "Christ-centered" universe. What do you think of this? Does this help or not help in your thinking about (a) Christ or (b) humanity? Why or why not?

2. Dante is often referred to as a "Christian humanist." Is that label confusing to you? Does it make more sense after having read this section? Would you refer to yourself in that way?

3. Do you think most humans are innately good? Do you think most humans are innately evil? Why did you answer as you did?

4. Do you think you yourself are a good person? (Be honest, now; if you think you are or are not a good person, go ahead and say so, at least to yourself and God.) Do you think you are a bad person? Why did you answer these questions as you did?

5. Do you think you could be easily corrupted? (Remember the Ring of Gyges?) Why or why not?

6. Look back over your answers to Questions 3-5. Would you have answered them differently before you became a Christian, or early on in your Christian experience? Why or why not?

References

1) The story is taken from Plato, *The Republic*. Book II.359-360. Translated by Francis MacDonald Cornford. Paperback edition. London: Oxford University Press, 1945: 44-ff.

2) John Calvin, *Institutes of the Christian Religion, Volume I*. Book II, Chapter 3, Section 3. Translated by Henry Beveridge. Grand Rapids, Michigan: Eerdmans Publishing, 1964: 252.

3) *The Republic*, Book II.360: 45.

4) *The Republic*. Book X.612: 347.

5) Russell Kirk, "The Peculiar Demesne of Archvicar Gerontion." *Watchers at the Strait Gate*. Sauk City, Wisconsin: Arkham House, 1984: 85.

6) Quoted in Paul Johnson, "The Necessity for Christianity." Updated July 14, 2002. leaderu.com.

7) Romans 2:14-15.

8) Genesis 1:27.

9) Romans 5:14-ff.

10) Romans 7:19, 24-25.

11) Quoted in Kent R. Rieske, "Total Depravity." 2004. biblelife.org.

12) Calvin, *Institutes, Volume I.* Book II, Chapter 3, Section 2: 250-51.

13) Book II, Chapter 3, Section 1: 250.

14) Book II, Chapter 3, Section 1: 248-49.

15) Guido de Bräs, "The Belgic Confession." Articles 14-15. reformed.org.

16) Romans 3:10-12.

17) Jeremiah 17:9.

18) Ephesians 2:1, 3.

19) Romans 3:16-18.

20) John 6:37, 44.

21) Romans 9:11-12, 15-16, 18-21.

22) Erik von Kuehnelt-Leddihn, "The Western Dilemma: Calvin or Rousseau." *Modern Age: The First Twenty-Five Years.* Indianapolis: Liberty Press, 1988: 525-529.

23) Kent R. Rieske, "Total Depravity." 2004. biblelife.org.

24) From Leon O. Hynson, "Original Sin as Privation: An Inquiry into a Theology of Sin and Sanctification." Edited by Michael Mattei. Wesley Center for Applied Theology, 2000. wesley.nnu.edu.

25) John Meyendorff, *Byzantine Theology: Historical Trends and Doctrinal Themes.* New York: Fordham University Press, 1979: 143-45.

26) In Augustine, *Ad Simplicianum.*

27) Paul Rigby, "Original Sin." *Augustine Through the Ages.* Edited by Allan D. Fitzgerald, O.S.A. Grand Rapids, Michigan: Eerdmans Publishing, 1999: 608.

28) Augustine, *Confessions and Enchiridion.* Translated and edited by Albert C. Outler. Philadelphia: Westminster Press, n.d.: 353-54.

29) Ludwig Ott, *Fundamentals of Catholic Dogma*. Translated by Patrick Lynch. Rockford, Illinois: TAN Books, 1974: 112-13.

30) Ronald B. Mayers, *Both / And: A Balanced Apologetic*. Chicago: Moody Press, 1984: 47.

31) Thomas Aquinas, *Compendium Theologica* I.75. *Light of Faith: The Compendium of Theology*. Translated by Cyril Vollert, S.J. New York: Sophia Institute Press, 1998: 71-72.

32) *Compendium Theologica* I.76: 72.

33) Thomas Aquinas, *Summa Theologica* I.22.4.

34) Isaiah 1:18.

35) Psalm 19:1-4.

36) Acts 14:17.

37) 1 Cor. 11:14.

38) John 1:9.

39) Acts 10:34-35.

40) Romans 1:19-20.

41) Romans 10:13.

42) Deut. 30:19.

43) Proverbs 1:29, 31.

44) Isaiah 7:15.

45) Ezekiel 18:27-28, 32.

46) Joshua 24:15.

47) 2 Cor. 5:17.

48) Ephesians 2:4-6.

49) Quoted in *C.S. Lewis: A Mind Awake*. Edited by Clyde S. Kilby. New York: Harcourt Brace Jovanovich, 1968: 21.

50) Ephesians 2:10.

51) Ephesians 1:6.

52) 2 Peter 1:4.

53) Robert Heilman, *Ghost on the Ramparts.* Athens, Georgia: University of Georgia Press, 1973: 165.

Chapter 6: Which Way Would Christ Vote?

"From the Christian vision of the human person there necessarily follows a correct picture of society."—Pope John Paul II, *Centesimus Annus* (1991).

"The president got re-elected [in 2004] by dividing the country along fault lines of fear, intolerance, ignorance, and religious rule. . . . drawing a devoted flock of evangelicals, or 'values voters' as they call themselves."—from a columnist.

"The election results reflect the decision of the right wing to cultivate and exploit the ignorance of the citizenry."—from a novelist.

"If militant Christianist Republicans from inland backwaters believe that secular liberal Democrats from the big coastal cities look upon them with disdain, there's a reason. We do, and all the more so after this election."—from a different columnist.

"America's political soul was in the grip of . . . the wacky religious right. Protecting the nation from their radical agenda requires our urgent prayers."—from a different novelist.

"The secular states of modern Europe do not understand the fundamentalism of the American electorate. . . . Where else do we find fundamentalist zeal, a rage at secularity, religious intolerance, fear of and hatred for modernity [except in radical Islam]?"—from yet another columnist.

"A small but significant, because articulate, sliver of the Democratic Party seems to relish interpreting the party's defeat as validation. This preening faction reasons as follows: the [2004 re-election] proves that 51 percent of the electorate are homophobic, gun-obsessed, economically suicidal, antiscience, theocratic dunces. Therefore to be rejected by them is to have one's intellectual and moral superiority affirmed."—from another columnist.

"You [on the left] missed no opportunity to profane their [Christians'] icons, to defile their society, to accuse them of bigotry, to

abolish their traditions, to strip their freedoms. At the same time, you demanded that they treat your own fetishes with the utmost sensitivity. You thought maybe it could go on forever?"—from another columnist.

"For the Democratic Party, churchgoing America is enemy territory."—from one more columnist.

"I have never been so blown away as by the totally opposite opinions Christians have on various [political] issues. Are we serving the same God? Are we even reading the same Bible?"—from a letter, *Charisma & Christian Life Magazine*, February 2005.

The *Kulturkampf*

It's no news that for the last several decades, the United States has been politically divided. Many have even spoken of this division in terms of a *Kulturkampf*, a "Culture War," an ongoing struggle to define American society. This war appears in numerous guises, but is waged especially ferociously in the bastions of cultural definition and trend-setting: the media, the entertainment industry, and the upper-level academy. (The church is not listed here, as it no longer functions as a trend-setter in society and hasn't for decades.) I was an undergraduate student at a large state university during the Reagan presidency, and I remember thinking at the time that the virulent hatred shown to Reagan in particular and conservatism in general by left-wing activist groups on campus could not conceivably be surpassed.

Boy, was I wrong.

In the 1990s, the country elected Democrat Bill Clinton to the White House for eight years, and the political temperature soared. The left already referred to the 1980s as the "Decade of Greed"; the right began referring to the 1990s as the "Decade of Denial." When I began teaching at a nearby college, my fellow teachers (who were for the most part rather predictably Democrats) and I would occasionally spar over whether Reagan or Clinton was more despised by his respective political opponents. Both sides of the debate had plenty of juicy anecdotes and war stories filled with the excesses of political rhetoric, name-calling, and opposition-bashing out on the extremes of the ongoing political battles, leading up to Clinton's impeachment and subsequent acquittal.

However, the political climate has changed even further, especially with the 2004 re-election of Republican George W. Bush for President. I don't think there is any question now as to who is the most hated recent President: Bush wins in a landslide. (I overheard an otherwise kind, good-hearted, and level-headed co-worker standing outside my office door say to another in complete seriousness, "I hope one of Bush's children dies, just to wipe that grin off his face." Without pause, the other person in the conversation said, "Oh, I do, too!" I am also sure these co-workers think of Republicans as the "mean-spirited" party.) On the other hand, Bush is also one of the most well liked people in the country, even going so far as to win a grudging Man of the Year award from *Time* magazine.

What is ominous and new about this division is that it has moved far inward from the "extremes" of political factionalism; most of the vast "middle ground" now is no longer "middle ground." It seems virtually everyone now holds his or her political opinions with an intimidating passion and vehemence, whether they are positive opinions or negative. On both sides, whether left or right, voting is seen as self-definition, as placing oneself in the camp of the righteous Children of Light as opposed to the evil Children of Darkness. The "red" and "blue" states marked off by television coverage of the 2000 and 2004 elections hit home with a particular resonance because we as a people have the uneasy sense that we are, in fact, becoming at least two separate nations. "Red" and "blue" labels slowly have become creepily reminiscent of "blue" and "grey." The "North" and "South" of previous divisions are now "the flyover states" and "the Coasts." If you doubt this, just ask yourself: If the citizens of Los Angeles, San Francisco, Seattle, New York City, and Boston were the only voters counted, how often would we have a Republican President? On the other hand, what if we only counted the votes of Dallas, Louisville, Tulsa, Omaha, and Salt Lake City?

Democratic vice-presidential nominee John Edwards may have been right when he spoke of the "two Americas." And one of the primary dividing lines in these "two Americas"—actually one of the most accurate predictors regarding national-election voting patterns—is religious belief and observance.

For example, in the 2004 presidential elections, the country's voters as a whole went for Bush by 51 percent to Democrat John Kerry's 48 percent. However, among those who attend church once a week, Bush received 58 percent of the vote. Among those who attend church more than once a week, Bush received 64 percent. Among Catholics Bush received 51 percent even while running against the first Catholic presidential candidate since 1960. Among white evangelicals, Bush received 78 percent.[1]

Not only do voting patterns vary according to religious commitment, but so also does the interpretation of those patterns. When faced with the statistics above, Group A reacts by proclaiming that religious conservatives are attempting to set up a theocracy, in which all Americans will be required to pledge allegiance to Jesus every morning before going off to their jobs as concentration-camp guards (non-union, of course). Group B, on the other hand, thinks of religious conservatives as fighting back against the intrusions of a cultural elite that wants to replace churches and synagogues with porn theaters, abortion mills, and crackhouses, while this elite pushes toward its ultimate goal of making gay marriage not just legal, but compulsory (and free for all minors).

I'm having a little fun here, of course. But isn't there enough truth in the caricature to make you stop and reflect? And notice that I didn't refer to "Christians" in the preceding paragraph, but "religious conservatives." What about religious non-conservatives? Where do they fit? It's a disquieting truth that liberal Christians seem to have more in common with liberal non-Christians, and conservative Christians with conservative non-Christians, than either Christian group has with the other. What happens to the testimony of Christ and the unity of Christ's Body when Christians are found in both Group A and Group B? Does one side hold the "real" Christians and the other side not? Is Christianity to be associated with a political party, and faith to become a variant of political philosophy? Should one Christian group demean and vilify another Christian group over political differences?

By the way, in case the reader thinks I am referring here only to Christian activism within the Republican Party, think again. The tendencies to identify one's religious convictions with a political group and to proffer one's political opinions with a sort of "Chosen People" moral certitude and superiority are just as prevalent in the Democratic Party as in any other. For every conservative fundamentalist in one party, there's an old-line denominationalist lefty in the other; for every Pat Robertson, there's a John Shelby Spong. And, to further muddy the cultural waters, some Christians promote politically liberal causes for theologically conservative reasons (Reinhold Niebuhr and Tony Campolo are two examples of this type).

The problem, however, is that all of these various Christians claim to be doing the work of righteousness, even as they work directly against the other. So we are left asking: Which actually is the work of righteousness? Which way would Christ vote?[2]

In the struggle to define American society and shape its priorities, both liberals and conservatives have set forth their claims to the moral high ground. (Even though some have claimed to be "beyond" the labels of liberal or conservative, I'm going to continue to use these terms, since the claim to be "beyond" such labels is itself a liberal characteristic. At least, you don't hear conservatives saying it.) Liberals accuse conservatives of:

- Insensitivity to the plight of—well, everyone, except those directly affected by higher capital-gains tax rates.
- Selfishness, as witness the still-repeated characterizations of the Reaganite '80s as a particularly "selfish" decade (even though charitable giving hit an all-time high during Reagan's presidency).
- Lack of compassion, coupled with a legalistic (and hypocritical) moral authoritarianism.
- Intrusion into issues of sexual privacy.
- Racism (for example, conservatives tend to oppose affirmative action quotas).
- War-mongering (when the President is a Republican).

Conservatives, on the other hand, accuse liberals of:

- The Gnostic rejection of reality, which primarily manifests itself as a willingness to spend others' money in the name of a utopian "compassion" which does not actually benefit its supposed beneficiaries.
- Injustice in dealing with the victims of crime.
- Moral laxness on "social" issues such as abortion and gay marriage, a laxness coupled with an infuriating moral smugness.
- Intrusion into issues of marital and family privacy (child-rearing decisions, for instance).
- Racism (for example, liberals tend to support affirmative action quotas).
- War-mongering (when the President is a Democrat).

These are serious charges in their own right. But notice that most of them can fundamentally be related to the respective views of human nature held by these disparate groups. I don't intend to rehash territory already covered in the previous chapter ("What Is a Human?"), but I do intend to build upon it. In that chapter, we discussed questions such as the nature of humanity—does it tend toward good or evil? Is it capable of almost unlimited possibilities in its elasticity or is it severely restricted by the bonds of sin? Should we be optimists or pessimists regarding the human condition? The conclusion reached was that we should think of humans in two different ways simultaneously: as fallen, mortal, and morally degraded, and yet also as created in God's image, possessing possibilities of freedom and non-material intellect almost divine in scope. However, these questions also need to be re-considered inasmuch as they seem to apply to that aspect of the human condition regimented and given direction by our *political* organization.

For example, liberals would perhaps not so optimistically declare a "War on Poverty" if they did not believe that the human condition was basically malleable, ripe for betterment through social engineering, and that we should seek to better the human condition whenever possible. On the other hand, conservatives would not so adamantly cling to states' rights and the separation of powers if they did not believe that centralized governmental power represents too strong a temptation to fallen human nature.

So it seems worthwhile to get beneath the ever-shifting intricacies of our ongoing political conflict and to bring the matter down to its most essential elements, down to its philosophical foundations, that is, down to religious questions. Let's bring the discussion to one question in particular:

Can we be faithful, biblical Christians and still go in different directions politically?

Questions for Reflection:

1. At this point, what's your answer to the question in the previous sentence?

2. Are there political issues which for you are non-negotiable when it comes to choosing a political candidate to support? What are those issues?

3. I have a friend who says she thinks of Christ as being completely non political. What do you think she means by this? Do you agree with her?

4. If you agreed with my friend (previous question), do you think the teachings of Christ have no political import and should not affect our political decisions? If you disagreed with my friend, do you think Jesus would be a Republican, a Democrat, or neither, if He lived in America today? Would Jesus vote at all? If you said no to that question: Why wouldn't He? Is the refusal to vote an avoidance of Christian responsibility?

5. Do you find it easier to fellowship with non-Christians who agree with you politically or with Christians who disagree with you politically?

6. Do you *have* any Christian friends who disagree with you politically? What is your opinion of their Christian commitment? Do their political views affect how you respond to that last question?

Gods and Devils

Let's approach some of these questions by beginning with an interesting and suggestive passage in John's Gospel related to the nature of humanity. In chapters 8-10, an extended discussion takes place between Jesus and the religious leaders opposing Him. Portions of this discussion follow (Jesus is speaking):

> "I know that you are descendants of Abraham; yet you seek to kill me, because my word finds no place in you. I speak of what I have seen with my Father, and you do what you have heard from your father."
> They answered him, "Abraham is our father." Jesus said to them, "If you were Abraham's children, you would do the works of Abraham. But now you seek to kill me, a man who has told you the truth which I have heard from God; this is not what Abraham did. You do the deeds of your father."

Then they answered him, "We were not born of fornication; we have one Father, even God."

Jesus said unto them, "If God were your Father, you would love me, for I proceeded forth and came from God; neither came I of my own accord, but He sent me. Why do you not understand my speech? It is because you cannot hear my word. *You are of your father the devil*, and the lusts of your father you will do. He was a murderer from the beginning, and abode not in the truth, because there is no truth in him. When he speaks a lie, he speaks according to his own nature, for he is a liar and the father of lies. But because I tell you the truth, you believe me not."[3]

The power of heritage and tradition, even a vital religious tradition, is never enough in itself to change the heart of a human. Jesus here points out a painful but essential truth: The nature of man is linked, as closely as a child to its father, to Evil. No matter how you interpret Christ's words here, they must at the very least give us a grim view of our fallen situation.

However, the argument between Jesus and the opposing religious leaders does not conclude with the hard-hitting blast of chapter 8. In fact, it continues through chapter 10 of John's Gospel, culminating in verse 30, where Jesus states, "I and my Father are one." This, of course, does not settle well with his opponents, who switch from argument to a more direct strategy:

Then the Jews took up stones again to stone Him. Jesus answered them, "Many good works have I shown you from my Father; for which of those works do you stone me?" The Jews answered Him, "For a good work we stone you not; but for blasphemy, because you, being a man, make yourself God."

Jesus answered them, "Is it not written in your law, 'I said, "You are gods"' [Psalm 82:6]? If he called them gods, unto whom the word of God came (and the scripture cannot be broken), do you say of Him, whom the Father has sanctified and sent into the world, 'You blaspheme,' because I said, 'I am the Son of God'?"[4]

Here, from the lips of Christ Himself, we once again perceive the paradoxical nature of the human being. We are capable of being called partakers of a devilish paternity, and at the same time, "gods" unto whom the Word of God has come both in written form and in the Incarnation of the Living Word, Christ. We are not merely creatures of the natural, clinging to life in this world only, but beings teetering between the demonic and the divine. Although natural beings, we are also part of a supernatural order which we apprehend through the combined forces of faith and reason. As C.S. Lewis has written, we enter this life as eating, sleeping, rutting animals, yet are commanded by God to imitate Him:

It is a serious thing to live in a society of possible gods and goddesses, to remember that the dullest and most uninteresting person you talk to may one day be a creature which, if you saw it now, you would be strongly

tempted to worship, or else a horror and a corruption such as you now
meet, if at all, only in a nightmare. . . . You have never talked to a mere
mortal.[5]

"What sort of freak then is man?" Pascal asks. "How novel, how monstrous,
how chaotic, how paradoxical, how prodigious! Judge of all things, feeble
earthworm, repository of truth, sink of doubt and error, glory and refuse of the
universe!"[6] Gods and goddesses, monsters and worms—our language rises to
poetic metaphor as we attempt to grapple with the nature of humans, to set forth
a sort of answer to the question: How could natural folks like you and me be
"gods" entrusted with the sacred Word of the Almighty, and yet linked in
intimate relationship to the devil? This is a "theological" question, of course,
and yet, as with all fundamental theological questions, its answer touches upon
every other aspect of human life and policy.

In fact, the people whom Christ here calls "gods" (Greek *theoi*, translated
from the Hebrew *elohim*) are not even living in the grace and knowledge of the
New Covenant; they are called "gods" simply by virtue of their covenantal
calling and assigned duties as representatives of God. In the context of Psalm
82, from whence Jesus is quoting, these are the judges of Israel, divinely
appointed but merely human, "condemned by the Great Judge for being unjust."[7]
Therefore, it seems that mortal man has been given a part to represent God
Himself and to exercise, at least in certain situations, even something of the very
authority of God. And God has chosen to act in this way in history—through
humans. We are thus called to such a dignity, such a partnership with the
Divine.

Can this "humanistic" belief in man's inherent possibilities as God's
representative be reconciled with a belief in man's corrupted and fallen nature?
Both beliefs seem biblically warranted; for example, in the Old Testament, the
view of humanity reveals that "man is not a brute, nor yet a half-demon of 'total
depravity'; his spirit's home is with God." This "exalted insight . . . is echoed so
often throughout the Old Testament that we can accurately assert it to be the
Hebraic understanding of man: a sinner capable of horrible brutalities, yet in his
true nature made in the image of God and partaking of the Divine mind and
nature."[8] This Jewish conception seems to be that of Jesus as well, as brought
out in the quoted passages from John's Gospel. However, liberal theologians
seem to emphasize the "goodness" of humanity while the more conservative
seem to emphasize humanity's "fallenness."

Perhaps a middle ground exists, such as political philosopher Glenn
Tinder's view that humanity is "sacred yet morally degraded." Tinder calls this
the "paradox at the heart of the Christian view of the individual—a paradox
unparalleled in secular outlooks but crucial in Christian political wisdom."[9]
Although humans are by nature fallible and prone to evil both in themselves and
in their institutions, they still retain a certain sacrality as spiritual beings made in
the image of God: "The individual who is fallen is nevertheless exalted."[10] To
quote Pascal once more:

It is dangerous to explain too clearly to man how like he is to the animals without pointing out his greatness. It is also dangerous to make too much of his greatness without his vileness. It is still more dangerous to leave him in ignorance of both, but it is most valuable to represent both to him.[11]

Tinder also points out that this is why equally committed Christians sometimes find themselves on opposite sides of political issues. One Christian sees the purpose of politics as helping to bring damaged mankind, made in the image of God, into closer approximation to that original image, and so he may take a more "liberal" view of the potential for political good to be achieved. Another Christian sees the purpose of politics as preserving hard-bought and delicately held institutions against the depredations of sinful human tendencies. This is the more "conserving" or "conservative" view. The first stresses the positive potential of humans, not in their own abilities but in their creation by God, while the second calls us to some rather grim and cautionary self-awareness. One views the world through the lens of Creation and the other through the lens of the Fall. Both outlooks having biblical validation, they must be held in some type of fruitful balance or tension, so that Christ cannot be so easily recruited to one pole or the other. And note well: When conservatives begin to highlight the potential for God's movement in human history through Christian political action, they are actually viewing politics through what I have called a "liberal" lens.

At any rate, both the recognition of man's innate potential capabilities and the recognition of his fallen nature are necessary for health and wholeness in personality and in Christian dialogue, including that peculiar type of dialogue known as the political. Only in recognizing both elements can we inculcate both the reformer's sense of urgency at the heart of true liberalism and the sense of the fitness and proper measure of things at the heart of true conservatism. Lacking one or the other, we become reactionaries or radicals.

All of this section so far has been background material, presented in order to reach this conclusion: Given all the above, it seems that equally faithful Christians could align themselves on opposite poles politically. It all depends on which particular aspect of Christ's redemptive mission is seen as crucial at any given moment in human history. The situations in Britain and the U.S. during the Christian movement to abolish slavery, for example, might have required a different political emphasis than the situations of those nations today. This isn't lack of principle or political opportunism, but political wisdom.

The primary virtues of genuine liberalism are respect for liberties and societal benefits, and the compassion to extend those liberties and benefits as far as possible. On the other hand, the primary virtues of genuine conservatism are gratitude and appreciation for the effort it takes to maintain hard-won existing institutions, and the love for future generations necessary to pass on those institutions. Whether or not one would be a politically liberal Christian or a politically conservative Christian would then depend on whether one thought the primary political duty of the historical moment would be the *reformation* or the *conservation* of society's institutions. An excellent example of this in contemporary life can be seen in the debate over "gay marriage." Think of your own position for a moment: Are you more inclined to think our marriage laws need *conservation* as they are, or need *reformation* to allow gay marriage? (I am a political conservative, by the way, because I see the overwhelming political need of the moment to be the conservation of the vulnerable institutions of civilization. What takes a hundred generations to build up can be destroyed in one, by neglect or direct attack or both.)

However, in one's thoughts on various matters of public policy, one could conceivably be both liberal in some areas and conservative in others at the same time, depending on the specific issues being addressed. Although this might just be the result of a lack of coherence in one's worldview, it might also be the result of a balanced and consistent faith. Is it our job to judge the Christian commitment of another by way of analyzing his or her political positions? What if both the drive to liberate and the drive to conserve come from one's Christian commitment?

This "balance" does not make Christ the patron of the lukewarm. He cannot in that sense of the word be called a moderate. Rather, He is at one and the same time both utterly liberal and utterly conservative. He inspires reform in those areas which require reformation and where it is possible at an appropriate cost, while He also inspires the protection of the worthy pillars of society so often underestimated in the reformer's terrible zeal. In all things Christ represents the perfect balance between realities set in tension. If then we would follow Him, we must also seek some like balance in all areas of human life and endeavor, including public policy and affairs of government.

We must also accept as fellow believers the faithful Christians who, in likewise seeking that balance, have arrived at different political commitments than our own. Political positions don't measure one's faith, on either side of the political divide.

Questions for Reflection:

1. I quoted Glenn Tinder as writing that the "paradox at the heart of the Christian view of the individual" is that humans are "sacred yet morally degraded." What do you think of this idea? How would you rephrase it in your own words?

2. I argue in this section that both "true" liberalism, the drive to liberate, and "true" conservatism, the drive to conserve, can come forth from the wellsprings of genuine Christian faith and commitment. Why do I say this? Do you agree or disagree?

3. "Political liberal" and "political conservative": Which label seems to you to fit more easily with "Christian"? Why? Do

you see any viable and worthwhile reasons for someone to consider himself or herself the other?

4. Earlier I asked whether or not we could judge the Christian commitment of another by way of analyzing his or her political positions. What is your answer to that question?

A Conversation Between Two Christians

I am greatly blessed in the people with whom I work. For example, Rhonda Eakins, a fellow teacher and now also Department Chair of the Arts and Sciences in our college, has been a close friend of mine for many years and has followed the chapter-by-chapter progress of this book with great interest and frequent contributions. As a Christian, she's an inspiration to all around her (though she would demur), and teaches the adult Sunday School in the United Methodist Church in the small town where she lives.

She is also a Democrat, while I am a Republican. Occasionally we get together for long conversations just so that I might persuade her of her essential wrongheadedness in this area, and so that she might persuade me I could be a better person if only I tried.

With Rhonda's permission, I'd like to present the highlights of some of our conversations. I'll focus on her views of the relationship between our Christian beliefs and political stances, while charitably restricting my own comments as much as I can:

Craig: You already know from our previous conversations most of what I've had to say in this chapter. You also know I consider myself a conservative and you a liberal, although you've told me you intensely dislike that label. Do you have any sort of opening comments?

Rhonda: Yes. The reason I dislike the labels "liberal" and "conservative" is because I think they're inaccurate. They don't really mean anything today. The Christian faith, as I think you've pointed out in this chapter, may be quite conservative culturally, and yet lead one in particular historical circumstances to political positions that may be thought of as "liberal." I don't think of myself as a moderate, either; I suppose if someone else were to examine my positions without knowing my motivations he might think of me as both liberal and conservative simultaneously.

Craig: But in order for people to think of your positions that way, the labels "liberal" and "conservative" must have meaningful content, correct?

Rhonda: I really don't think they do. They may have at one time, but their definitions have changed and shifted so often, they can be misleading by now. At any rate, the overall label "liberal" does not accurately describe what I am or how I think. For example, there are some basic points I think we both would agree upon: First, we both think that our political beliefs and actions cannot be separate from our Christian beliefs. We shouldn't be double-minded, and the fact of being a Christian comes first in everything. Wouldn't a politically conservative Christian say basically the same thing?

Second, faith issues do have a place in public discourse, out in the naked public square, as Richard John Neuhaus puts it, and cannot be relegated to the "private sphere" alone.

Third, because we believe in absolute standards, we believe God's moral requirements are for the benefit of all people, and are not just "religious rules" that apply only to those who share our Christian faith.

Fourth, we agree that Christian core values, such as the sanctity of life and the obligation to act justly and mercifully, have implications for public policy.

Craig: By "obligation to act justly," do you mean the obligation to render to people what they need or to render to them what they deserve?

Rhonda: Well, we could agree on either of those definitions and still disagree as to what people *qua* people need or deserve.

Craig: How about the obligation to act mercifully? How is that to be codified politically? If it is codified, it's no longer mercy, but law.

Rhonda: If we codify morality, does that make it no longer morality?

Craig: It makes it law. Someone could behave morally based on fear of the law rather than on a love for the good. I wouldn't call that a genuine morality, since it doesn't arise out of an autonomous decision to behave morally. It doesn't even have to know what *is* right or wrong. It just does what it's told.

Rhonda: But the motivation of fear of the law and obedience to the law does not automatically exclude the motivation of love for the good, does it?

Craig: No.

Rhonda: All right; then the same could be true of mercy. It is still a Christian obligation to seek to infuse God's mercy into all arenas. Again, we might agree on the obligation but disagree as to how specifically it is to be practiced. It's quite possible for Christians to share a core belief and yet disagree on how that belief should be translated into public policy. Feeding the hungry, for example: one Christian might see a larger purpose for the government in this, while another might think the government is creating a permanent underclass, or that the first Christian is trying to abdicate responsibility for the poor by foisting it off onto the government. Now perhaps one of them has a better or more workable solution than the other, but that doesn't mean that one has the Christian answer and the other doesn't.

God looks at our hearts. He knows if our motivations for political action are in accord with his will. Even a good policy with a wrongful motivation is not a "Christian" policy. God's kingdom is not political, though we Christians have often tried to make it so. If we think we can establish his kingdom by legislative or other political means, we are wrong. Both the right *and* the left are guilty of this, I recognize and admit, since I sense you're itching to point it out to me. The body of Christ is not "Red" and "Blue," so we shouldn't use political litmus tests to determine which party is the "Party of God." Both parties can be wrong at times and right at times.

Look at Matthew, who would have been viewed as a Roman collaborator, and Simon the Zealot, who would have been vehemently and perhaps violently opposed to Roman rule—yet they were both followers of Jesus and worked together. (This idea is not original with me, by the way. I think it comes from Jacques Ellul.) I don't necessarily think the public perceptions of the Republican Party are fair or accurate, but I do think that we have identified evangelical Christianity with the agenda of that party. Some people may be driven away from the faith if we are so closely aligned with one side. I am certain the Book of Life is not taken from voter registration lists.

Craig: You mentioned "litmus tests." Aren't there some issues that automatically rule out a vote for the party endorsing them? If one side actively seeks to promote acceptance of abortion-on-demand, for instance, or assisted euthanasia (or physician-mandated euthanasia, as some European countries are now discussing), wouldn't pointing out their good or even Christian qualities be rather like saying, "Pol Pot was really a decent person except for the genocide thing"?

Rhonda: You know that I am pro-life. I agree that we cannot be "pro-choice" if we believe in the sanctity of human life. This would seem to make the choice of political parties quite clear. But I'm not sure it is that clear. Many Democrats are actually pro-life, though the official position of the party is pro-choice, just as many Republicans go against the official position of their party by being pro-choice.

Craig: You're right about the last part, but I challenge you: I'll name ten prominent pro-choice Republicans for every one prominent pro-life Democrat you can name—an office-holder, I mean. Can you name even one?

Rhonda: I'm referring to Democrats at the local caucus level. There's a lot more diversity on that issue than you might think.

Craig: Yes, but that means you have to accept that you have absolutely no influence over your party on the national level. Democrats in national office are monolithically pro-choice.

Rhonda: If I thought switching from the Democratic Party to the Republican would end abortion, restore the sanctity of marriage, and stem the tide of moral degeneracy in this country, I would change parties in a second. But I don't believe it would happen. I'm not sure the Republican Party is really committed to ending abortion. Despite that party's being in power for much of the last thirty years, abortion rights are as strong as ever. I think much of the problem is that Republicans in leadership positions simply use pro-life rhetoric to pacify and solidify a political base. If Democrats should leave their party because of the pro-choice plank, then Republicans should also leave their party for years of rhetoric rather than action.

Craig: And then?

Rhonda: After that, I don't know. I suppose that's the reason we are both staying where we are and fighting to transform our parties from within.

Craig: You mentioned the sanctity of human life as a concept in opposition to the pro-choice position. Can a Christian be pro-choice?

Rhonda: Well, I think so—but he or she would be mistaken in being so. Intellectually, the pro-life position has won. There are no pro-choice arguments I know of that haven't been refuted by pro-life arguments rather decisively. But communicating that case to the general public is another matter entirely, and is complicated by our self-loving and convenience-loving natures. By the way, I know Republicans who are pro-choice because abortion disproportionately eliminates the under-class, and because it also disproportionately eliminates children (future voters) who would otherwise be born into Democratic families. And I know a lot of people who are pro-choice because they really do not know the full extent and latitude of U.S. law in this area. So yes, a person can be a Christian and still not have a real understanding either of the pro-life or pro-choice position.

Craig: What would be a deciding factor for you to leave the Democratic Party?

Rhonda: If what I can accomplish for the sake of Christ's kingdom within the Democratic Party no longer outweighs the negatives of staying, I would leave. But couldn't I ask you the same about the Republican Party? What if it turns out your party's official positions on social issues are just lip-service?

It's possible I am entirely wrong about this; however, it's not something I haven't thought about extensively. And, of course, I still think about it all the time.

Craig: I'll let you have the last word.

Rhonda: Thank you.

I am a sincerely committed follower of Jesus Christ (not always a very good one, I'll admit, but one who sincerely desires to do what is pleasing to God). I want nothing more than my whole life to be a testament to Christ. "Christian" is the most important label I have, more important than "wife" or "mother" or "teacher," and infinitely more important than any political label.

To have someone question the reality of my faith simply because of a political affiliation is not just offensive; it is hurtful and destructive. I think it was a conservative Republican who once wrote that 90 percent of our political arguments are not 10 percent as important as we think they are at the time. Even if some think I am wrong in some of my commitments—we are still one spirit and one family in the Lord. That's what is most important, above all else on earth.

* * *

Let me close with a quote Rhonda pointed out to me, from Philip Yancey's book *The Jesus I Never Knew*:

> The issues that confront Christians in a secular society must be faced and addressed and legislated, and a democracy gives Christians every right to express themselves. But we dare not invest so much in the kingdom of this world that we neglect our main task of introducing people to a different kind of kingdom, one based solely on God's grace and forgiveness. Passing laws to enforce morality serves a necessary function, to dam up evil, but it never solves human problems. If a century from now all that historians can say about evangelicals of [our time] is that they stood for family values, then we will have failed the mission Jesus gave us to accomplish: to communicate God's reconciling love to sinners.[12]

Just one more quote, please:

> A society that welcomes people of all races and social classes, that is characterized by love and not polarization, that cares most for its weakest members, that stands for justice and righteousness in a world enamored with selfishness and decadence, a society in which members compete for the privilege of serving one another—this is what Jesus meant by the kingdom of God.[13]

Questions for Reflection:

1. Rhonda listed four areas of agreement between Christians across the political spectrum in this section:

-   Our political beliefs and actions cannot be separate from our Christian beliefs.
-   Faith issues do have a place in public discourse and cannot be relegated to the "private sphere" alone.
-   Because we believe in absolute standards, we believe God's moral requirements are for the benefit of all people, and are not just "religious rules" that apply only to those who share our Christian faith.
-   We agree that Christian core values, such as the sanctity of life and the obligation to act justly and mercifully, have implications for public policy, even though we may disagree on their specific applications.

Here's my question: Do you think there actually is Christian agreement in these areas? Why or why not?

2. When we hear politicians on television demanding economic
    and social "justice," the word "justice" may be used in at least
    two different ways: as meaning what people *need* to have or as
    meaning what people *deserve* to have. One definition stresses
    basic provision, while the other stresses accountability. Which
    better fits your own definition of "justice"? How would these
    different definitions lead to different views on public policy?
    Which definition do you think is a more "Christian" view of
    justice? Are they both "Christian"? Why or why not?

3. What is your view of the intelligence of those who disagree
    with your political views? What is your inner attitude toward
    them personally?

4. I know I've asked you this before, but one more time won't
    hurt: What is your view of the spirituality and Christian
    commitment of those who disagree with your political views?

References

1) Don Feder, "Christians Eat Lions." *The American Enterprise.* Jan. / Feb. 2005: 12.

2) Some of the following material is taken from Craig Payne, "Whose Side Is Christ
On?" *Touchstone: A Journal of Ecumenical Orthodoxy.* 4.4 (Fall 1991): 11+.

3) John 8:37-45, emphasis added.

4) John 10:31-36.

5) Quoted in *C.S. Lewis: A Mind Awake.* Edited by Clyde S. Kilby. New York: Harcourt
Brace Jovanovich, 1968: 125.

6) Blaise Pascal, *Pensées.* Translated by A.J. Krailsheimer. Taken from Peter Kreeft,
Christianity for Modern Pagans: Pascal's Pensées *Edited, Outlined, and Explained.* San
Francisco: Ignatius Press, 1993: 108.

7) Willem A. VanGemeren, *Psalms. The Expositor's Bible Commentary, Volume 5.*
Edited by Frank Gaebelein. Grand Rapids, Michigan: Zondervan, 1991: 534. Although
VanGemeren himself disagrees with the interpretation given (i.e., the "gods" as Israel's
judges), it is supported by several sources (Vincent's *Word Studies*, Vine's *Expository
Dictionary*, Calvin's *Commentaries*, Keil and Delitzsch's *Commentary on the Old
Testament*, etc.).

8) William A. Irwin, "Creation." *Hastings' Dictionary of the Bible.* Edited by James Hastings. Revised edition edited by Frederick C. Grant and H.H. Rowley. New York: T. & T. Clark and Charles Scribner's Sons, 1963: 187.

9) Glenn Tinder, *The Politics of Christianity.* 1st paperback edition. New York: HarperCollins, 1991: 35.

10) *The Politics of Christianity*: 42.

11) Pascal, *Pensées.* Taken from Kreeft, *Christianity for Modern Pagans*: 52.

12) Philip Yancey, *The Jesus I Never Knew.* Grand Rapids, Michigan: Zondervan, 1995: 247.

13) *The Jesus I Never Knew*: 253.

Chapter 7: Left Behind

"Two men walking up a hill, one disappears, and one's left standing still,
I wish we'd all been ready.
There's no time to change your mind; the Son has come and you've been left
behind."—from the song "I Wish We'd All Been Ready," by Larry Norman.[1]

Will You Be Left Behind?—book title.

The Second Coming of Jesus Christ Already Happened—book title.

"I once believed that there were two types of prophecy enthusiasts—those
who shared my views . . . and those who had not yet heard them convincingly
presented. . . . I had not been made aware of any responsible alternatives to my
own view. . . . I was aware only that some Christians were so unfortunate as to
set the Rapture of the church at a time different from that in my system. It was,
therefore, unsettling to me when my own studies in Scripture began to confront
me with details and implications that challenged my interpretive
conclusions."—from an evangelical Bible school professor.

"[Christ] sitteth on the right hand of the Father; and He shall come again,
with glory, to judge both the living and the dead; whose kingdom shall have no
end. . . . And I look for the resurrection of the dead, and the life of the world to
come. Amen."—from the Nicene Creed.

"God returns all the time and begins time."[2]

The Hope of Christ's Coming

At one time in my Christian life, my maturity level was low, my walk of
love was close to nonexistent, and my faith was probably more presumptuous
than not. It's a good thing I had solid Christian mentors and several strong
Christian friends to help carry me along. However, I at least had one thing going
for me, or so I thought: I was absolutely certain the Rapture of the Church was
going to take place in 1981, and I was ready to go.

My rationale for this was simple: Most Christians I knew believed that
Jesus' apocalyptic teaching in Matthew 24 covered a seven-year "Great Trib-

ulation" period. This seven-year period came after a great "catching-away" event referred to as the Rapture of the Church (from the Latin *rapare / rapio*, comparable to the Greek *parousia*). Jesus had said, "This generation shall not pass, till all these things be fulfilled."[3] A biblical generation was roughly forty years, and the "generation" I thought Jesus was pointing toward was the generation seeing Israel's re-establishment as a nation. Israel had been re-established as a nation in 1948; forty years added onto that brought us to 1988. In order for "all these things" to be fulfilled, the Great Tribulation had to be finished by that time. Therefore, seven years of Tribulation subtracted from 1988 took us back to 1981, the year of the Rapture. *Quod erat demonstrandum.*

Only it didn't happen. Perhaps we'd miscalculated. At least we thought so when two books came out by previously unknown writer Edgar Whisenant, books that sold close to five million copies: *On Borrowed Time* and especially *88 Reasons Why the Rapture Could Be in 1988*. Whisenant was quite confident about the 1988 date, and specified even further that the Rapture would take place between September 11 and September 13 (Rosh Hoshanah) of that year. "Only if the Bible is in error am I wrong," he proclaimed, "and I say that to every preacher in town." During one interview he said, "If there were a king in this country and I could gamble with my life, I would stake my life on Rosh Hoshanah 1988" (as the time for the Rapture to take place).[4] Likewise, prophecy teacher Hal Lindsey, whose 1970 work *The Late Great Planet Earth* had been a phenomenal best seller, a decade later released *The 1980s: Countdown to Armageddon*. That book declared on its cover, "The decade of the 1980s could very well be the last decade of history as we know it."[5]

Only, again, it didn't happen.

Then we decided that the year 2000 (Y2K) was the year of Christ's returning. Again, there was a biblical reason: According to Genesis 1, there were six days of creation and then one day of rest. There had been four thousand years of human history from Adam to Christ, and two thousand from Christ to Y2K, more or less (although the mistaken sixth-century calendar of Dionysus Exiguus made our numbering rather inexact). This six thousand years of history corresponded to the six days of creation, and now it was time for the "day of rest," the thousand-year Millennial reign of Christ's established kingdom upon earth. After all, as we often quoted, didn't the Bible say that a thousand years of human history was as a day with the Lord?[6] Also, the so-called "Y2K Bug" was supposed to crash computer systems worldwide, leading to devastation and panic throughout the world's population. At that point the earth would experience its greatest revival, as it would be prepared for our Christian witness by its traumatic experiences.

It might be difficult at this remove to remember the anxiety and speculation of the days leading up to the year A.D. 2000. I recall one minister saying in a nation-wide broadcast, "How close is the Rapture? Well, I'll tell you one thing—don't buy any green bananas." People stockpiled food and water and purchased generators for the emergency supplies thought to be required. Likewise it might be difficult to remember the combined relief and disappointment when again nothing happened. And even today (in the year 2005) I heard a minister on television arguing that the Y2K calculations were essentially correct and that God in his mercy is only granting "a sliver of time" before the Rapture takes place. Other ministers are equally sure of the shortness of time remaining in human history; as one writes:

> As we approach the Seventh Millennium [this was published in 1997], time seems to have accelerated and prophetic events are being compressed together. We have entered the triangle of the end [that is, if human history were shaped like a triangle, we would now be entering the narrow point at the apex], in which both the time allotted and prophetic events are being compressed to maximum density to fulfill all the prophetic Scriptures, and end the age in God's own time frame. . . . We are spiraling faster and faster through the narrow end of the triangle of time, for the purpose of being released into a new Millennium that will forever change planet earth.[7]

Later in the same work, the author says, "Get prepared for the most traumatic change that will ever come to this planet in six thousand years. There is no doubt about it. We are in the end-time harvest. It is the season of His appearing."[8]

So we've had the dates 1981, 1988, and 2000 given for the Lord's return—and that's only within my personal memory! When we look further back in Christian history, we find Christian apocalyptics who expected the end of the world in the year A.D. 1000; Joachim of Fiore, who thought the world was about to end in the twelfth century; Christopher Columbus, who in part desired to expand the reach of Christianity because of his belief the world would end in the 1500s; Martin Luther and other reformers, who believed the Protestant Reformation was an end-time fulfillment of prophecies in the book of Revelation, with the papacy in the role of the Antichrist; various groups who looked for and specifically predicted Christ's return in the 1830s, the 1840s, the 1960s, and the 1970s; and the list could go on and on.

However, the specific teachings on a "pre-tribulation Rapture" as presented in today's church actually began in the 1820s with Edward Irving, a Scottish clergyman whom even supporters referred to as "rather unstable" and "eccentric," but "spiritually sensitive."[9] These teachings then were primarily promoted beginning in the years 1827-1830 by John Nelson Darby, a British minister of the Plymouth Brethren. In 1859 Darby also began teaching in the United States, in particular presenting his system of "dispensationalism":

> Darby taught that God has dealt with mankind in a series of epochs, or dispensations. . . . One cycle of prophesied events ended with Jesus' crucifixion; the next will begin with the *Rapture*—the moment when all believers will rise to meet Christ in the air. Once the prophetic clock begins ticking again with the Rapture, the final sequence of events will unfold with dismaying rapidity for those left behind, beginning with the seven-year reign of Antichrist and the Apostate Church, the so-called *Tribulation* (Matt. 24:21), of which the second half will be sheer hell. . . . The Tribulation will end with the

Battle of Armageddon, when Christ, the saints, and the heavenly host return to earth and defeat Antichrist and his army. Next will come the *Millennium*, Christ's thousand-year rule on earth; a final, doomed uprising by Satan; the resurrection of the dead; and history's final event, the Last Judgment.[10]

This has become by far the best-known and most popular system of prophecy interpretation in the United States today. After Darby's ministry, dispensationalism received widespread currency by the 1909 publication of C.I. Scofield's *Scofield Reference Bible*, with Scofield's own extensive annotations and footnotes. "The line of continuity from Darby can be traced through W.E. Blackstone, G. Campbell Morgan, H.A. Ironside, A.C. Gaebelein, and C.I. Scofield to more recent times," writes professor of history Robert G. Clouse, editor of *The Meaning of the Millennium*. "Dispensationalism has become the standard interpretation for over 200 Bible institutes and seminaries in the United States. Many famous interdenominational evangelists including D.L. Moody and Billy Graham have also adopted this understanding of eschatology [the study of end-time events]."[11] Students of this system typically maintain that the symbolic images of Matthew 24, the Book of Daniel, and the Book of Revelation are closely related to each other and often linked to current events in world history.

Occasionally pre-tribulationists try to show Rapture teaching as existing in previous centuries of the Church age (before the 1800s), but are for the most part lacking evidence of this; for example, a single sentence from an Orthodox sermon by "Pseudo-Ephraem," probably dating from around A.D. 700, is sometimes cited.[12] Pre-tribulationist Herbert VanderLugt argues in response to this problematic lack of early evidence that "the early church fathers and their successors did not establish a systematic doctrine of last things":

> The writings of the early church fathers have been quoted by both pretribulationists and posttribulationists as supporting their position. After reading a large number of these quotations, I am convinced that these early church fathers did not teach pretribulationism as we understand it. But neither did they set forth a distinctive posttribulation view. . . . They have little bearing on the issues that divide Bible scholars on this controversial doctrine.[13]

In our own day, interest in pre-tribulational Rapture teaching is evidenced by the sales of the fictional *Left Behind* series, co-authored by minister Tim LaHaye and writer Jerry B. Jenkins. As of this writing, the series has sold about 70 million books, making LaHaye and Jenkins America's best-selling authors. Roughly one out of every eight Americans has read at least one of the novels in the twelve-volume series. Somewhat surprisingly, according to research done by Tyndale, the novels' publisher, "More Jews, agnostics, and atheists read the series than mainline Protestants":

> And why are so many people eager to do that? Well, check the news tonight. As the world gets increasingly scary, with much of the trouble centered in the Mideast—just where you'd expect from reading the Book of Revelation—even

secular Americans sometimes wonder (or at least wonder if they ought to start wondering) whether there might not be something to this End Times stuff. . . . And it's no coincidence that the books are a favorite with American soldiers in Iraq.[14]

"Many of us thought that the coming and going of Y2K and the beginning of a new millennium would cause people to question dispensational assumptions and preoccupations with signs of the end," writes pastor and teacher Kim Riddlebarger. He goes on: "However, the success of the *Left Behind* series of end-time novels . . . proves the influence and staying power of dispensational teaching."[15]

Despite dispensationalism's popularity, however (especially in America), the question increasingly is arising: Is dispensationalism the only honest interpretive stance a believing Christian can hold regarding the end-time scriptures? Are the doctrines of the Rapture, Great Tribulation, Antichrist, Second Coming, Millennial Reign of Christ, and Final Judgment (sometimes called the "Great White Throne" judgment, from Rev. 20:11) so immediately apparent from our reading of the Scriptures that one must accept them all or else be regarded as unfaithful to God's Word?

If one answers these questions "Yes," then, as we've already discussed, one must also regard most of the historical Christian Church as blinded with respect to the "immediately apparent" interpretation of biblical prophecy. The Church has always held to its belief in Christ's judgment of the righteous and unrighteous, the resurrection of the dead, and life everlasting with God in eternity. But the teaching of the Rapture of the Church is notably absent from the Church's historical consensus. In early post-New Testament literature such as the Didache, the Epistles of Barnabas and Clement, Justin Martyr's "Dialogue With Trypho," and the "Vision" of the Shepherd of Hermas, Christians are described as eagerly awaiting the Lord's return, "looking for that blessed hope, and the glorious appearing of the great God and our Savior Jesus Christ"[16]—but awaiting this blessed hope as a Second Coming, *after* they have passed through their time of tribulation, not as a special Rapture to rescue them *from* their tribulation. As one writer says:

> The hope of the Church throughout the early centuries was the second coming of Christ, not a pretribulation rapture. If the Blessed Hope is in fact a pretribulation rapture, then the Church has never known that hope through most of its history, for the idea of a pretribulation rapture did not appear in prophetic interpretation until the nineteenth century. . . . To deduce from [the Church's] attitude of expectancy a belief in a pretribulation rapture and an any-moment coming of Christ, as has often been done, is not sound.[17]

In fact, there are at least four basic views of biblical prophecy that have been held and promulgated by Christians as being both scriptural and validated in history. These four views, the Futurist (which we have already been considering), the Historicist, the Symbolist, and the Preterist, all still have able defenders even today. I'd like to turn now to an examination of these four views (while refraining from promoting one or the other), with the aim in mind of demonstrating that equally faithful Christians have scriptural warrant for holding different views on the end-times teaching of the Bible.

In other words, the complex of Rapture-oriented dispensationalist teachings referred to collectively as the "Futurist" position, despite its popularity and the fact of its being the best known eschatological stance in America, is not necessarily a teaching believers have to believe.

Questions for Reflection:

1. I mentioned the Futurist position of belief in the pre-Tribulation Rapture, Great Tribulation, Antichrist, Second Coming, Millennial Reign of Christ, and Final Judgment. How much of this corresponds with prophetic teachings you have heard? How much of it corresponds with what you yourself believe?

2. Have you ever heard of the other prophetic interpretive positions mentioned (Historicist, Symbolist, Preterist)? What have you heard?

3. If a minister holds a different interpretation of biblical prophecy than you do, would you trust what that minister has to say on any other topic? Why or why not?

Four Views of New Testament Prophecy

Prophecy teaching and prophecy seminars are quite popular among a very large segment of contemporary Christianity. People are fascinated by the heightened oracular power of the prophetic scriptures and the sense of special insight or "behind-the-scenes" information that is unveiled (as in the Greek term *apocalupsis*, "revelation" or "unveiling"). But because of this special power and insight, and because many prophecy teachers believe their message to be of paramount importance in our day, the in-fighting between those of differing views may wax especially bitter.

For example, when Tyndale House, the publisher of Tim LaHaye's *Left Behind* novels, also published Hank Hanegraaff's *The Last Disciple* (a fictional interpretation of the book of Revelation from the Preterist point of view), LaHaye became openly angry. "They are going to take the money we made for them and promote this nonsense," LaHaye said about Tyndale's release of the book by Hanegraaff, who is best known as host of the "Bible Answer Man" radio program. "I feel the whole evangelical community has been betrayed by a major publisher that, for forty years, has been a stalwart of biblical interpretation based on a literal interpretation of the scriptures; and now they're advancing a book that destroys literalism in favor of an allegorical interpretation of history. I don't know what science fiction he [Hanegraaff] is reading." In response to the "science fiction" remark, LaHaye's own novels were described as "futuristic" and "speculative" by Sigmund Brouwer, Hanegraaff's co-author of *The Last Disciple*.[18] In contemporary Christianity, the intensity of arguments over the future seems to be rivaled only by that of arguments over the pre-historic past (see Chapter 3 of this book).

In fact, despite the dense imagery and allusive character of most biblical prophetic texts, many Christian teachers seem to regard their own interpretations as more or less self-evident and other interpretations as fanciful and speculative. "I once believed that there were two types of prophecy enthusiasts—those who shared my views . . . and those who had not yet heard them convincingly presented," writes evangelical Bible school professor Steve Gregg:

> I had not been made aware of any responsible alternatives to my own view (out of charity to my teachers, I will assume that they were likewise unaware). I was aware only that some Christians were so unfortunate as to set the Rapture of the church at a time different from that in my system. It was, therefore, unsettling to me when my own studies in Scripture began to confront me with details and implications that challenged my interpretive conclusions. . . . I became aware of radically different approaches to [biblical prophecy] that made at least as much sense as did mine. Some of these views had been around much longer than mine.[19]

The view originally held by Gregg was a form of Futurist dispensationalism. Note well that he does not describe dispensationalism as unbiblical, nor as not making sense. Nor does he say that he abandoned the Futurist position. All he says is that other views "made at least as much sense." For a student and teacher of biblical prophecy, this is a major concession indeed.

So what are these "radically different approaches" to New Testament prophecy? In addition to the Futurist view, three others have already been mentioned. Here follows a brief definition and history of all four:

- **Futurist:** Futurists believe that almost all New Testament prophecy (for example, chapters 4 through 22 of the Book of Revelation) is still to be fulfilled in the future—hence the name "Futurist." Futurists typically believe in a future catching away of Christian believers (the Rapture of the Church), in which Jesus returns "in the clouds" but technically not "to the earth"; a revived European Roman Empire ruled over by a literal person who will be the Antichrist; and a seven-year Great Tribulation over the earth. At the conclusion of the seven years, Jesus will return again with the previously raptured believers and destroy his enemies in the climactic Battle of Armageddon; this is the "Second Coming," in which Jesus actually returns "to" the earth. (Sometimes the Rapture and this event are referred to as the first and second "stages" of the

Second Coming.) The Second Coming will usher in a thousand-year reign of peace called the Millennium. At the end of the Millennium, Satan will be released from confinement to tempt humanity once more; following this comes the Resurrection of the Dead and their Final Judgment. Satan will be bound and punished eternally, the heavens and earth will be literally re-created, and humans will be divided into those spending eternity with God and those going to Hell. To reiterate: Since they believe that these are the events primarily described by New Testament prophecy, Futurists also believe almost all New Testament prophecy is as yet unfulfilled. This is probably the most popular interpretation of biblical prophecy in America today, especially among evangelical and Pentecostal Protestants.

- **Historicist:** Historicists believe that New Testament prophecy is in the process of being fulfilled throughout history, with some already behind us and some yet to occur. This was the most popular method of interpreting prophecy in Protestant Christianity from the time of the Reformation (the 1500s) until the mid-1800s. For example, Martin Luther saw the Book of Revelation as an ongoing picture of Christian and world history, with the Pope as the Antichrist and the Roman Catholic Church as the Harlot of Babylon, destined (according to Rev. 17) to be overthrown. (Some Historicists believe a partial fulfillment of this prophecy took place during and immediately after the French Revolution, as the Roman Catholic Church in Europe lost much of its prestige and power.) While some elements of prophecy are yet to be fulfilled in the future, Historicists typically do not believe in a future Rapture of the Church. Although the Historicist view is the least popular today, notable Christians who have held it in one form or another include Luther, John Wycliffe, John Knox, Ulrich Zwingli, John Calvin, Isaac Newton, Jonathan Edwards, Charles Finney, Matthew Henry, Adam Clarke, and Charles Spurgeon.[20]

- **Symbolist:** Typically the Symbolist does not relate New Testament prophecy to any specific time frame at all. This approach "does not attempt to find individual fulfillments of the visions but takes [New Testament prophecy] to be a great drama depicting transcendent spiritual realities, such as the spiritual conflict between Christ and Satan, between the saints and the antichristian world powers, and depicting the heavenly vindication and final victory of Christ and his saints. . . . [P]rophecy is thus rendered applicable to Christians in any age."[21] Every day and always, in other words, Christians must face tribulation and the Antichrist world system, but biblical prophecy gives us ongoing encouragement and reveals our ultimate victory in Christ the King—it is spiritually *representative* rather than historically *predictive*. Theologian J.A.T. Robinson provides an example of this approach; he "interprets Christ's parousia not as a literal event of the future but as a symbolical . . . presentation of what happens whenever Christ comes in love and power. . . . Judgment day is a dramatic picture of every day."[22] In the words of another Christian professor and writer, "The challenge of [Jesus'] unexpected prophecies is to accept the transforming rapture ever and again."[23] Many Roman Catholics and mainline denominationalist Protestants hold this view.

- **Preterist:** Like Futurists and Historicists, and unlike Symbolists, Preterists also believe in the literal fulfillment of New Testament prophecy within historical events. However, they believe that most or all New Testament prophecy was fulfilled in the generation of the early church, at the destruction of Jerusalem in A.D. 70. "Partial" preterists believe that the final judgment and resurrection of the dead are still in the future.[24] "Total" preterists (sometimes called proponents of a "realized eschatology") believe that *all* prophecy, including the Judgment and Resurrection, occurred at the coming of the Lord in judgment against Jerusalem.[25] Sometimes this view is amended with the idea that the "resurrection" of every believer occurs at the time of that believer's death, with death's concomitant release into an eternal spiritual life. "Thus the fulfillment [of biblical prophecy] was in the future from the point of view of the inspired [biblical authors], but it is in the past from our vantage point in history."[26] So the book of Revelation, for example, was written sometime prior to Jerusalem's fall in A.D. 70, rather than at approximately A.D. 95 (the date maintained by most Futurists); noted Christians who favor this early dating include Adam Clarke, J.B. Lightfoot, Philip Schaff, and J. Stuart Russell ("perhaps the most important scholar of the preterist school"[27]), as well as the majority of Bible scholars in the 1800s. Therefore, when New Testament writers spoke of the "soon" return of Christ, they meant it literally—Jesus actually did return within the lifetime of their readers, if we understand his "coming" as a "coming in judgment" to Jerusalem, a judgment against those rejecting Him and a deliverance of those serving Him.

For some readers, this may be the very first time they have become aware of these interpretive options. These readers may feel more comfortable with one or two of these options than with the others. However, before they dismiss as "fanciful" any views contrary to their own, they may consider these words:

"[N]one of these schools of interpretation can claim any monopoly on scholarship or faith. Each group numbers many fine scholars and devout Christian believers. . . . It is our duty to do the best we can, to study the various systems and accept the view that seems to us right, but always with a certain amount of reservation and of respect for the opinions of others."[28] This seems not only reasonable, but Christian.

Questions for Reflection:

1. Are there any aspects of prophetic teaching all four views seem to hold in common? What are they? What are the teachings over which the four views definitely disagree?

2. Having read the definitions provided for these four views of biblical prophecy, are there now any of them about which you'd like to learn more? Why or why not? If so, which ones?

3. Look back over the past few years: How important has biblical prophecy been in your own life? Would you say you've spent more time discussing biblical prophecy with Christian friends or discussing the claims of Christ with non-Christian friends?

A Look at Matthew 24 and the "Left Behind" Passage

Earlier I wrote that I planned to refrain from promoting one of these positions or another. However, I'm reasonably confident that most of the readers of this book are more aware of the Futurist dispensationalist position than of any other; not only is it the best known in America, but it is also the most "noticeable." It's a teaching that gets headlines: "Christians Say Rapture Could Occur at Any Moment" grabs the attention much more readily than "Christians Say All History Is Part of God's Plan" or "Christians Say Prophecies Fulfilled in A.D. 70: Massive Amounts of Detailed, Small-Print Argumentation to Follow." Even non-Christians would think the second headline to be rather banal, while the third would cause immediate glazing-over of the eyes.

So, since the Futurist position is already fairly well known, in this section I want to allow a less familiar position, the Preterist, to speak for itself. Let's imagine a conversation between a Futurist and a Preterist. As the Preterist position will require more background explanation, I will let the Preterist do most of the talking, with the Futurist making comments and offering criticisms.

A focal point of interpretive dispute among biblical prophecy experts is the Olivet Discourse, Jesus' words as recorded in Matthew 24 and its parallel passages, Mark 13 and Luke 17 and 21. An analysis of this one prophecy might be enough to get a taste of the differences in the two interpretive stances.

Therefore, this imagined conversation will revolve around the single chapter of Matthew 24, the verses of which I will interpolate as needed:

> [1] And Jesus went out, and departed from the temple: and his disciples came to him to show him the buildings of the temple.
> [2] And Jesus said unto them, See ye not all these things? verily I say unto you, There shall not be left here one stone upon another, that shall not be thrown down.
> [3] And as he sat upon the mount of Olives, the disciples came unto him privately, saying, Tell us, when shall these things be? and what shall be the sign of thy coming, and of the end of the world?

Preterist: It seems like a simple enough question.

Futurist: But it is not. If you'll notice, there are actually two questions. "The order is as follows: 'When shall these things be?'—i.e., destruction of the Temple and city. . . . The remainder of Matthew 24:3 really constitutes a single question: 'And what shall be the sign of thy coming, and of the end of the age [*aion*, translated as "world" in the King James Version]?' The answer [to this second question] is in verses 4-33."[29] So Jesus' followers are asking Him to explain first of all what He meant by saying the Temple would be destroyed; secondly, they are asking Jesus to reveal the signs of his future coming. Matthew 24 answers two separate questions, in other words. One question's answer (the destruction of the Temple) has already occurred in history, while the other's (the coming of Jesus) is yet to come.

Preterist: There are at least a couple of reasons I wouldn't accept your argument. First, the disciples do not seem to be concerned with a coming of Christ in the far future—this is really one question, not two. When Jesus tells them the Temple will be destroyed, they respond rather naturally by assuming the destruction of the Temple is an act of judgment by the coming Messiah, Who is standing in front of them. The "end of the age" is not the end of all history, but the end of the Jewish system of Temple worship and sacrifice. Worship is from henceforth to center around the new Temple, Jesus' body, broken and raised up in three days.[30] The Temple's destruction, the Messiah's coming in judgment on Jerusalem, and the end of the Temple age—all of these events are wrapped up in one question with one answer.

Secondly, I wouldn't accept your argument because Jesus gives the disciples a very straightforward, literal answer to their single question. They ask when these things will happen. He begins answering them by telling them what to expect, and then summarizes in verse 34: "Verily I say unto you, This generation shall not pass, till all these things be fulfilled." He tells them that all the prophecies of Matthew 24, at least up to verse 34, will be fulfilled in their generation.

Futurist: No, the "generation" Jesus is talking about in verse 34 is not the generation of people then living. It is either (1) the generation of people seeing the Rapture, or more likely (2) the "race" of Jews (from the Greek *genea*). He is simply saying that the Jews *as a people* would not pass away until all these prophecies were fulfilled, despite all the intense persecutions of the Jewish *genea.* "The record of history validates our Lord's words. For the Jews have survived despite the Torquemadas, the Hitlers, the Stalins, and the Eich-manns."[31] The Jewish people will still be around to see the fulfillment of Jesus' words; that is what He is saying to them.

Preterist: That seems a very strained and unnatural reading of that verse. Every-where else in Matthew's Gospel, *genea* is used for the generation then alive. For example, from the previous chapter:

> Verily I say unto you, all these things shall come upon *this generation.* O Jerusalem, Jerusalem, thou that killest the prophets and stonest them that are sent unto thee, how often would I have gathered thy children together . . . and ye would not! Behold, your house is left unto you desolate.[32]

" 'This generation' is a recurring phrase in the Bible, and each time it is used it bears the ordinary sense of the people belonging to one fairly comprehensive age group. . . . Jesus' hearers could have understood Him to mean only that 'all these things' would take place within *their* generation. Not only does 'gener-ation' in the phrase 'this generation' always mean the people alive at one particular time; the phrase itself always means 'the generation now living.' "[33]

If we understand the "coming" of the Lord as a coming in judgment to those who rejected Him, then verse 34 carries a literal meaning. Jesus spoke these words in about A.D. 30, and Jerusalem and the Temple are destroyed by the Roman general Titus beginning with the extensive siege of A.D. 70—within the generation of those then alive, in other words, just as Jesus predicted. "Forty years is not too long a period to be called a generation; in fact, forty years is the conventional length of a generation in the biblical vocabulary."[34] This also explains a later incident: "As Jesus bears his cross to Calvary He exhorts the 'daughters of Jerusalem' to weep for themselves because of the coming judgment."[35] He has already predicted what is going to happen *to them*, not to a generation in the distant future.

In fact, He has already told his followers the exact same thing previously, that the generation hearing Him would be the generation seeing his coming: "But when they persecute you in this city, flee ye into another: for verily I say unto you, Ye shall not have gone over the cities of Israel, till the Son of man be come."[36] Doesn't that sound like a literal prediction of a first-century return of Christ?

Futurist: There are several problems with your literal reading of verse 34 and "this generation." However, in order to highlight these problems, we'll have to look at some more selections from Matthew 24 itself.

Preterist: All right.

> [4] And Jesus answered and said unto them, Take heed that no man deceive you.

[5] For many shall come in my name, saying, I am Christ; and shall deceive many.
[6] And ye shall hear of wars and rumors of wars: see that ye be not troubled: for all these things must come to pass, but the end is not yet.
[7] For nation shall rise against nation, and kingdom against kingdom: and there shall be famines, and pestilences, and earthquakes, in diverse places.
[8] All these are the beginning of sorrows.
[9] Then shall they deliver you up to be afflicted, and shall kill you: and ye shall be hated of all nations for my name's sake.
[10] And then shall many be offended, and shall betray one another, and shall hate one another.
[11] And many false prophets shall rise, and shall deceive many.
[12] And because iniquity shall abound, the love of many shall wax cold.
[13] But he that shall endure unto the end, the same shall be saved.
[14] And this gospel of the kingdom shall be preached in all the world for a witness unto all nations; and then shall the end come.

Futurist: Here's the first problem with your view that Matthew 24 is for the most part fulfilled in the first century church: Look at verse 14. Has "all the world" heard the gospel preached? Even today, we wouldn't say the entire world has heard the gospel as a witness, and it certainly could not have been true in the first century. What about the peoples of Africa, China, Southeast Asia, and the Americas, just to name a few? When did the first-century apostles preach the gospel to them? So we see that the promise "and then shall the end come" is still to be fulfilled in the future.
Preterist: No, the "end" of which Jesus speaks is still the end of Temple worship at the destruction of Jerusalem under Titus.
Futurist: Your interpretation *cannot* be correct, as I've already pointed out, because the whole world could not have heard the gospel in the first century of the church.
Preterist: Yes, it did.
Futurist: Okay, now you're joking, right?
Preterist: Not at all. First, the word for "world" that Jesus uses is not the more typical Greek *kosmos* (the ordered creation) or *aion* (age, eon). Rather, He uses *oikoumene*, which means "land" or "the inhabited terrene world." To be even more precise, *oikoumene* means "specifically the Roman Empire," according to Strong's *Concordance.*[37] The same word is used in Luke 2:1, "And it came to pass in those days, that there went out a decree from Caesar Augustus, that *all the world* should be taxed." This certainly does not refer to all the "earth" (South America, Australia, Africa, etc.), but all lands within the purview of the Roman Empire.

In his translation of the New Testament, Kenneth Wuest even renders Matthew 24:14 as "And there shall be proclaimed this good news of the kingdom in the whole Roman Empire." Of course, since Wuest is a Futurist, he immediately adds in brackets, "the whole Roman Empire [the future revived empire].["38] However, it's much more probable that Jesus was simply referring to the Roman Empire of the first-century church.

According to many biblical passages, the Roman Empire of the first century *did* hear the gospel before A.D. 70. "These that have turned the world [*oikoumene*] upside down have come hither also," cried out the Thessalonians.[39] Paul told the Roman church, "Your faith is spoken of *throughout the whole world*,"[40] and wrote further of this triumphant witness elsewhere in his letters:

- ". . . according to my gospel, and the preaching of Jesus Christ, according to the revelation of the mystery, which . . . now is made manifest, and . . . *made known to all nations* for the obedience of faith."[41]
- ". . . be not moved away from the hope of the gospel, which ye have heard, and which was *preached to every creature* which is under heaven."[42]
- "For the hope which is laid up for you in heaven, whereof ye heard before in the word of the truth of the gospel: which is come unto you, as it is in *all the world*, and bringeth forth fruit, as it doth also in you."[43]
- "But I say, Have they not heard? Yes verily, their sound went into *all the earth*, and their words unto *the ends of the world* [*oikoumene*]."[44]
- And so on.

So it seems legitimate to interpret the prophecy of Jesus literally. The gospel would be preached to all the Roman Empire (all the *oikoumene* world), and then the end (of Jerusalem and the Temple) would come. Adam Clarke comments, "When this general publication of the Gospel shall have taken place, then a period shall be put to the whole Jewish economy, by the utter destruction of their city and temple."[45] This is what Jesus means when He says, "And then shall the end come."

In fact, this view helps explain the next few verses of Matthew 24:

[15] When ye therefore shall see the abomination of desolation, spoken of by Daniel the prophet, stand in the holy place (whoso readeth, let him understand),
[16] Then let them which be in Judea flee into the mountains:
[17] Let him which is on the housetop not come down to take any thing out of his house:
[18] Neither let him which is in the field return back to take his clothes.
[19] And woe unto them that are with child, and to them that give suck in those days!
[20] But pray ye that your flight be not in the winter, neither on the sabbath day:
[21] For then shall be great tribulation, such as was not since the beginning of the world to this time, no, nor ever shall be.

[22] And except those days should be shortened, there should no flesh be saved: but for the elect's sake those days shall be shortened.

Preterist: Jesus is specifically warning the people of Judea, the observant Jews who would keep the Sabbath day, that they would face "great tribulation" very soon. However, He also points out in verse 22 that some of the Jewish people would make it through those horrible days. The "abomination of desolation" is also explainable as a first-century event; in fact, the parallel to this passage in Luke's Gospel records Jesus as saying Jerusalem's "desolation" occurs when the city is "compassed with armies,"[46] probably a prediction of the siege of Titus.

Futurist: Look, the promise of the imminent coming of Christ is a great help in motivating Christians to witness to the unsaved world before the end comes. Given your description of a "first-century coming," what happens to that motivation in the present-day church?

Preterist: I don't think anything necessarily has to happen to our motivation. Why couldn't we have the same motivation the early church had: the motivation that people need salvation, that the unsaved should hear of God's redeeming love in Christ, and that our love constrains us to reach out?

Futurist: All right, but that's not my primary objection to your position, anyway. You've done an ingenious job of explaining away these prophetic truths, but . . .

Preterist: I'd rather think of it as "explaining" instead of "explaining away."

Futurist: At any rate, let me point out a much different linking together of these scriptures. The Christian church of today is preaching the gospel to all the world and will round out that task, "looking for and hastening the coming of the day of God."[47] At that (future) point, the end shall come and Jesus Christ shall return for his saints. After Jesus catches away his church, the "abomination of desolation" will then be set up by the Antichrist in the restored Temple as prophesied in the Book of Daniel, and a ferocious persecution of the Jews will ensue, during which many will flee into the wilderness areas of Israel. We find out elsewhere (not here in Matthew) that this "great tribulation" will last for seven years. After this, in the next few verses of Jesus' prophecy in Matthew 24, we see the next great event in God's prophetic timetable—the Second Coming of the Lord:

[23] Then if any man shall say unto you, Lo, here is Christ, or there; believe it not.

[24] For there shall arise false Christs, and false prophets, and shall show great signs and wonders; insomuch that, if it were possible, they shall deceive the very elect.

[25] Behold, I have told you before.

[26] Wherefore if they shall say unto you, Behold, he is in the desert; go not forth: behold, he is in the secret chambers; believe it not.

[27] For as the lightning cometh out of the east, and shineth even unto the west; so shall also the coming of the Son of man be.

[28] For wheresoever the carcass is, there will the eagles be gathered together.

[29] Immediately after the tribulation of those days shall the sun be darkened, and the moon shall not give her light, and the stars shall fall from heaven, and the powers of the heavens shall be shaken:

[30] And then shall appear the sign of the Son of man in heaven: and then shall all the tribes of the earth mourn, and they shall see the Son of man coming in the clouds of heaven with power and great glory.

[31] And he shall send his angels with a great sound of a trumpet, and they shall gather together his elect from the four winds, from one end of heaven to the other.

[32] Now learn a parable of the fig tree; When his branch is yet tender, and putteth forth leaves, ye know that summer is nigh:

[33] So likewise ye, when ye shall see all these things, know that it is near, even at the doors.

[34] Verily I say unto you, This generation shall not pass, till all these things be fulfilled.

[35] Heaven and earth shall pass away, but my words shall not pass away.

[36] But of that day and hour knoweth no man, no, not the angels of heaven, but my Father only.

Preterist: Wouldn't this be a "Third Coming" according to your view, since Jesus already came back previously in the Rapture?

Futurist: No. In the Rapture (which I think of as the "first stage" of the Second Coming), Jesus comes for his church, but does not actually return "to" the earth.

Preterist: I think that's a semantic quibble, but I'll let it pass.

Futurist: We also see in this passage another reason why I cannot accept your position on these prophecies. In verse 27, the return of Christ is described as "lightning." And especially look at verses 29-30, where Jesus describes the sun as darkened, the moon not giving light, the stars falling from heaven, the powers of the heavens shaken, and especially all the earth seeing the Son of man coming in the clouds of heaven with great glory. I take these words as a literal description of end-time events according to Jesus Himself—and none of them has happened yet. Have these atmospheric signs occurred yet? Did "all the tribes of the earth mourn" and "see" the coming of Jesus "in the clouds of heaven" at the destruction of Jerusalem? We must respond in the negative, to both of these questions. So we know that at least these events certainly didn't happen in the first century. However, I imagine you'll now argue that they did.

Preterist: That's correct; I think they did occur. You see, Jesus is ministering in the tradition of the Hebrew prophets, who often used the exact same imagery that Jesus uses here to describe God's judgment on a civilization or on a specific city or area. For example, the prophets often described the Lord as "coming in the clouds" to deal with his enemies[48]:

- In Isaiah: "The burden of Egypt. Behold, the Lord rideth *upon a swift cloud*, and shall come into Egypt: and the idols of Egypt shall be moved at his presence, and the heart of Egypt shall melt in the midst of it."[49]

- In Jeremiah: "Behold, *He shall come up as clouds,* and his chariots shall be as a whirlwind. . . . O Jerusalem, wash thine heart from wickedness, that thou mayest be saved."[50]
- In Ezekiel: "For the day is near, even the day of the Lord is near, *a cloudy day*; it shall be the time of the heathen. . . . At Tehaphnehes also *the day shall be darkened*, when I shall break there the yokes of Egypt: and the pomp of her strength shall cease in her: as for her, *a cloud* shall cover her. . . . Thus will I execute judgments in Egypt: and they shall know that I am the Lord."[51]
- In Nahum: "God is jealous, and the Lord revengeth; the Lord revengeth, and is furious; the Lord will take vengeance on his adversaries, and He reserveth wrath for his enemies. The Lord is slow to anger, and great in power, and will not at all acquit the wicked: the Lord hath his way in the whirlwind and in the storm, and *the clouds are the dust of his feet*."[52]

According to the *Dictionary of Biblical Imagery*, "Clouds serve as God's war chariot in the imagination of the Old Testament poets and prophets. . . . One of the most pervasive images of Christ's return is as one who rides his cloud chariot into battle."[53]

So when Jesus says that the tribes of the earth "shall see the Son of man coming in the clouds of heaven with power and great glory," He means the nations will witness the stunning destruction of Jerusalem in A.D. 70, when the Lord comes in the clouds for judgment. Jesus is not talking like a television weather reporter predicting some rather odd conditions, but He *is* talking like Isaiah, Jeremiah, Ezekiel, and Nahum—like a biblical prophet, in other words.

Futurist: So you only think of Jesus' words as "imagery" rather than as reality?

Preterist: Your "imagery / reality" distinction is a false dilemma. "Imagery is not meant to be taken literally, but it *is* meant to be taken seriously."[54] Jesus is using a serious image, an image of coming destruction and ruin. He's not talking about a cloudy day; He's talking about events that are really going to occur in the lives of his first-century hearers.

The disturbances of the sun, moon, and stars are also common images found in the prophets. "In the prophetic language, great commotions upon earth are often represented under the notion of commotions and changes in the heavens"[55]:

- The fall of Babylon is represented by the stars and constellations of heaven withdrawing their light, and the sun and moon being darkened (Isaiah 13:9-10).
- The destruction of Egypt is represented by the heaven being covered, the sun enveloped with a cloud, and the moon withholding her light (Ezekiel 32:7-8).

- The destruction of the Jews by Antiochus Epiphanes is represented by casting down some of the host of heaven, and the stars to the ground (Daniel 8:10).
- And this very destruction of Jerusalem is represented by the prophet Joel (Joel 2:30-31) by showing wonders in heaven and in earth—darkening the sun, and turning the moon into blood.

"This general mode of describing these judgments leaves no room to doubt the propriety of its application in the present case [i.e., in Matthew 24]."[56] The Lord coming in the clouds, the sun, moon, and stars being darkened, the powers of the heavens being shaken—all this took place at the Lord's coming in judgment upon Jerusalem, in A.D. 70.

Futurist: Here we see a good example of what John Walvoord describes in his commentary on the Book of Revelation: "The Preterist view, in general, tends to destroy any future significance of [biblical prophecy], which becomes a literary curiosity with little prophetic meaning."[57] What meaning do Jesus' words have for believers today if, as you say, these prophecies have been fulfilled for two millennia already?

Preterist: I don't think Walvoord's comment is necessarily accurate. Look at Isaiah 53, for example, the prophecy of the Suffering Messiah: Most Christians think that particular prophecy has already been fulfilled in the sacrificial crucifixion of Christ. However, just because Isaiah's words are already fulfilled does not take away any part of their significance for us, since they reveal Jesus more fully to us as our great Redeemer. Likewise, even if Jesus' prophetic words in Matthew 24 have already been fulfilled, they still have significance for us. They reveal Jesus to us even more fully as the Lord of all the earth and the great Judge of the nations.

Let's look at one more section of Matthew 24, the passage dealing specifically with those who are "left behind":

[37] But as the days of Noah were, so shall also the coming of the Son of man be.

[38] For as in the days that were before the flood they were eating and drinking, marrying and giving in marriage, until the day that Noah entered into the ark,

[39] And knew not until the flood came, and took them all away; so shall also the coming of the Son of man be.

[40] Then shall two be in the field; the one shall be taken, and the other left.

[41] Two women shall be grinding at the mill; the one shall be taken, and the other left.

[42] Watch therefore: for ye know not what hour your Lord doth come.

Futurist: Yes, this is a wonderful passage. At this point Jesus reiterates his central message: Be on the alert at all times, for the catching away of the church could occur at any moment, and you don't want to be one of those "left behind."

Preterist: Well, here's one thing on which we can agree: Christians should always be on the alert for the moving of God in their lives and circumstances, for we don't want to be "left behind" in his purposes and dealings. However, in context, this "left behind" passage, contrary to the series of novels by that name, is not referring to a catching away of the church.

This seems obvious just from a cursory reading of the text. Jesus says that his coming will occur "as in the days of Noah"; He further points out that the people judged by God in the days of Noah "knew not until the flood came, and took them all away." In other words, it is *the people who are judged* who are "taken away" to judgment and death, and the righteous Noah and his family who are "left behind" on the earth—those "left behind" are spared from judgment! In the parallel passage in Luke's Gospel, the disciples immediately ask Jesus a natural question: "Where, Lord?"—i.e., "Where will those taken away be taken?" Jesus replies, "Wheresoever the body is, thither will the eagles [vultures] be gathered together."[58] However you interpret this (for instance, it could be a reference to the armies of Rome surrounding Jerusalem like vultures at a kill), it certainly cannot be interpreted as the joyous, celebratory occasion of the church being caught up to reign with Christ eternally.

So, thanks to the recent series of novels, here we have the most famous passage in the New Testament regarding the Rapture of the Church—and it doesn't really refer to the Rapture at all!

Futurist: Before you confuse the issue any further, let me offer an alternate interpretation and an objection. First, when Jesus refers to those "left behind" and those "taken away"—even in the case of Noah and his world—He does not mean the judged were "taken away" to judgment and Noah and his family were "left behind" to be spared. He means Noah was "taken away" *from* judgment, and the rest were "left behind" *to face* judgment. So LaHaye's *Left Behind* novels are indeed titled entirely appropriately. Those not going in the Rapture will be "left behind" to face tribulation.

That's the alternate interpretation. Here's the objection: You say that Jesus' words here do not refer to the Rapture of the Church even while you call his words "the most famous passage in the New Testament regarding the Rapture." But even that is an arguable point. What about Paul's words to the Thessalonians:

> For the Lord Himself shall descend from heaven with a shout, with the voice of the archangel, and with the trump of God: and the dead in Christ shall rise first: then we which are alive and remain shall be caught up together with them in the clouds, to meet the Lord in the air: and so shall we ever be with the Lord.[59]

Even if Jesus' prophecy in Matthew's Gospel does not completely spell out all end-time events, there are other passages in the New Testament (such as this one) that you cannot explain away with a first-century fulfillment. These verses clearly describe a yet-future catching away of the church.

Preterist: I still don't think so. In order to rightly understand Paul's words here in First Thessalonians, you have to understand first of all that . . .

* * *

Sorry, but I'll have to cut in here and allow the prophetic discussion to continue elsewhere, as it doubtless will, in other books and other venues. However, I think the main point has been made: People with widely different interpretations of biblical prophecy can be equally faithful to Scripture and to the cause of Christ. As Steve Gregg has put it, I can recognize that other views make "at least as much sense" as does mine, and that different interpretations of biblical prophecy do not attempt to "explain away," but to explain.

I would be the last to minimize our Blessed Hope. The Nicene Creed tells us that Christ "shall come again, with glory, to judge both the living and the dead," and that his kingdom "shall have no end." Christians are to "look for the resurrection of the dead, and the life of the world to come." *Maranatha*—"Our Lord comes," according to the New Testament.[60] However, believing in Christ's Coming does not necessitate believing in it in one specific form or another.

Christ can come to translate us out of tribulation and prevent its occurrence in our lives. His power can also come to take us *through* tribulation if necessary. In fact, every day Jesus comes to us, in the Word and in the Spirit, to lift us into his eternal realm of blessedness, to lead us into further triumph. His coming does not divide his body, but unites it. "God returns all the time and begins time." In all situations and at all times this blessed hope fills our hearts.

Questions for Reflection:

1. If you are a Preterist, do you think the Preterist position was presented adequately in this section? Is there anything you would have said differently?

2. If you are a Futurist, do you think I should have given the Futurist position more space for explanation? Do you think your position was explained adequately? Is there anything you would have said differently?

3. If you do not yet hold any specific position on biblical prophecy, did this discussion help your understanding? Did it *not* help? Why or why not? Toward which position do you now lean? Why?

4. If the Rapture of the Church occurs exactly as described by the Futurist position, do you think your Christian brothers and sisters who do not believe in the Rapture will be "caught away"? Or will they be "left behind"? Why do you think this?

5. *Maranatha*—Our Lord comes. (P.S. If I say I believe this with all my heart, what exactly does that mean to you?)

References

1) "I Wish We'd All Been Ready." Words and music by Larry Norman. From the album *Only Visiting This Planet*. Solid Rock Productions. Copyright 1969.

2) From the poem "An Enemy Is Reliable," by Joy Lyle. Used by permission of the author.

3) Matthew 24:34.

4) Taken from "Field Guide to the Wild World of Religion." isitso.org.

5) Hal Lindsey, *The 1980s: Countdown to Armageddon*. New York: Bantam Books, 1980: frontispiece and cover.

6) Psalm 90:4.

7) Charles Capps, *End-Time Events: Journey to the End of the Age*. Tulsa: Harrison House, 1997: 20.

8) *End-Time Events*: 246.

9) Herbert VanderLugt, *Perhaps Today! The Rapture of the Church*. Grand Rapids, Michigan: Radio Bible Class, 1984: 85-86.

10) Paul Boyer, *When Time Shall Be No More: Prophecy Belief in Modern American Culture*. Cambridge: Belknap Press of Harvard University Press, 1992: 87-88.

11) Robert G. Clouse, "Foreword." In Steve Gregg, *Revelation: Four Views*. Nashville: Thomas Nelson, 1997: xiv.

12) For one of the better presentations of the attempt to find belief in a pre-tribulation Rapture in the early Church Fathers, see Thomas Ice, "The Myth of the Origin of Pretribulationism." pre-trib.org.

13) *Perhaps Today! The Rapture of the Church*: 85, 87.

14) David Gates, "The Pop Prophets." *Newsweek* 24 May, 2004: 46-47.

15) Kim Riddlebarger, *A Case for Amillennialism: Understanding the End Times*. Grand Rapids, Michigan, and Leicester, England: Baker Books and Inter-Varsity Press, 2003: 10.

16) Titus 2:13.

17) George Eldon Ladd, "The Historic Hope of the Church." From *The Blessed Hope.* Grand Rapids, Michigan: Eerdman's, 1980. groups.msn.com/ChristianEndTimeViews.

18) John Draper, "*Left Behind* Co-Author Slams Contrary New Series." christian-retailing.com.

19) Steve Gregg, *Revelation: Four Views.* Nashville: Thomas Nelson, 1997: 1.

20) *Revelation: Four Views*: 34.

21) *Revelation: Four Views*: 2-3.

22) Taken from F.F. Bruce, "Eschatology." *The Evangelical Dictionary of Theology.* Edited by Walter A. Elwell. Grand Rapids, Michigan: Baker Books, 1984: 364.

23) Robert Jewett, *Jesus Against the Rapture: Seven Unexpected Prophecies.* Philadelphia: Westminster Press, 1979: 142.

24) For an example of the "partial" preterist position, see Kenneth Gentry's *Before Jerusalem Fell.* Tyler, Texas: Institute for Christian Economics, 1989; or Larry T. Smith's *The Coming of the Lord, the Last Days, and the End of the World.* El Campo, Texas: Rightly Dividing the Word, 2000.

25) For an example of the "total" preterist position, see Max King's *The Cross and the Parousia of Christ.* Warren, Ohio: Parkman Road Church of Christ, 1986.

26) Steve Gregg, *Revelation: Four Views*: 2.

27) R.C. Sproul, *The Last Days According to Jesus.* Grand Rapids, Michigan: Baker Book House, 1998: 24.

28) Albertus Pieters, *The Lamb, the Woman, and the Dragon.* Grand Rapids, Michigan: Zondervan, 1937: 42.

29) C.I. Scofield, footnote to Matthew 24:3, *New Scofield Reference Edition.* New York: Oxford University Press, 1967.

30) John 2:18-21.

31) Dr. Walter Martin, *Essential Christianity: A Handbook of Basic Christian Doctrines.* Revised edition. Ventura, California: Regal Books, 1980: 97.

32) Matthew 23:36-38.

33) F.F. Bruce, *The Hard Sayings of Jesus.* From *Hard Sayings of the Bible,* by Walter C. Kaiser, Jr.; Peter H. Davids; F.F. Bruce; and Manfred T. Brauch. Downers Grove, Illinois: InterVarsity Press, 1996: 446.

Left Behind 137

34) F.F. Bruce, from *Hard Sayings of the Bible*: 447.

35) Kenneth Gentry, *Before Jerusalem Fell*: 130.

36) Matthew 10:23.

37) *Oikoumene* is entry 3625 in the "Greek Dictionary of the New Testament" section of James Strong, *Strong's Exhaustive Concordance of the Bible*. 34th printing. Nashville: Abingdon Press, 1976.

38) Kenneth Wuest, *The New Testament: An Expanded Translation*. Grand Rapids, Michigan: Eerdmans Publishing, 1961.

39) Acts 17:6.

40) Romans 1:8.

41) Romans 16:25-26.

42) Col. 1:23.

43) Col. 1:5-6.

44) Romans 10:18.

45) Adam Clarke, *Commentary on Matthew*. In *Parallel Classic Commentary on the New Testament*. Edited by Mark Water. Chattanooga, Tennessee: AMG Publishers, 2004: 339.

46) Luke 21:20.

47) 2 Peter 3:12.

48) The following examples are taken from Larry T. Smith, *The Coming of the Lord, the Last Days, and the End of the World*: 14-15.

49) Isaiah 19:1.

50) Jeremiah 4:13-14.

51) Ezekiel 30:3, 18-19.

52) Nahum 1:2-3.

53) "Cloud," from the *Dictionary of Biblical Imagery*. Edited by Leland Ryken, James C. Wilhoit, and Tremper Longman III. Downers Grove, Illinois: InterVarsity Press, 1998: 157.

54) Peter Kreeft and Ronald K. Tacelli, *Handbook of Christian Apologetics*. Downers Grove, Illinois: InterVarsity Press, 1994: 308.

55) This and the following scriptural examples are taken from Adam Clarke, *Commentary on Matthew*. In *Parallel Classic Commentary on the New Testament*: 343.

56) Adam Clarke, *Commentary*: 343.

57) John F. Walvoord, *The Revelation of Jesus Christ: A Commentary*. Chicago: Moody Press, 1966: 18.

58) Luke 17:37.

59) 1 Thes. 4:16-17.

60) 1 Cor. 16:22.

Part 3: Grace and Peace

Chapter 8: What Believers Don't Have to Believe

"O my God, Light of my eyes in darkness, since I believe in these commandments and confess them to be true with all my heart, how can it harm me that it should be possible to interpret these words in several ways, all of which may yet be true? How can it harm me if I understand the writer's meaning in a different sense from that in which another understands it? . . . . Do you not see how foolish it is to enter into mischievous arguments which are an offense against that very charity for the sake of which he wrote every one of the words that we are trying to explain?"—Augustine, *Confessions*.

"Given the fatuities peddled in the name of Christianity, one would prefer not to be a Christian, were it not true."—Richard John Neuhaus.[1]

"We are ignorant of essentials because we deal in non-essentials."—Seneca.

"We would be in the best shape if we kept in essentials, Unity; in non-essentials, Liberty; and in both Charity."—Peter Meiderlin, c. A.D. 1625.

Our Inheritance

In the early stages of the writing of this book, I had a visit from Joel, a former student, now studying theology elsewhere. He listened carefully as I described the chapter I was working on (it happened to be Chapter 4, on the inspiration of the Bible), and then commented thoughtfully, "So—are you sure you're not just lining up opposing quotes from one famous Christian after another? Are you trying to show that any point of view is possible if it has been held by at least some Christian somewhere?"

This misapprehension was quickly corrected. However, there was enough of a germ of truth in these questions to cause discomfort. So let me point out why I do think of Joel's questions as revealing a certain misunderstanding:

- Not every point of view is equally plausible. Throughout this book, my emphasis has been to maintain the primacy of the Scriptures, the Christian understanding of the Scriptures as preserved in the standard confessional Creeds, and the consensus of the majority of Christians throughout history.
- Even if a viewpoint has been held by a Christian, even a famous and highly respected Christian, it very well may not be an orthodox Christian teaching. Again, throughout this book, I've argued for the doctrines that have been held "always, everywhere, and by all," as Vincent of Lérins has it. However, I am willing to allow for a wide variation in belief and teaching, as long as we don't insist that any non-essential beliefs within this variation are in fact crucial for considering ourselves Christians. These non-essential beliefs, of course, are what comprise the central section of this book, the matters believers "don't have to believe."

But Joel wasn't finished with me yet. "So," he asked again, "are you arguing that correct Christian doctrine depends on majority rule? Is Christianity a democracy?"

Well, again, there is enough truth in that question to give it bite. Certainly God's commands are commands, not suggestions for us to debate and vote on, and his Word is a declaration, not a philosophical argument. Further, throughout history the majority has in fact been wrong on occasion and the minority correct.

However, my ultimate answer to Joel was "Yes." We should have:

- Enough humility to respect those doctrines the believing Church has consented to assert, argue for, and preach.
- Enough humility to accept correction if necessary.
- Enough humility to accept that our "pet" doctrines and teachings may not actually be all that important in the larger scheme of the Christian life.

The studied reflection of thousands of Christians throughout history, what Chesterton calls "the democracy of the dead," cannot be casually dismissed under the "inspiration" of the moment. We should at least consider that there were *reasons* for those traditional doctrines held by the Church, even if we do not always immediately perceive them.

Of course, we cannot live solely by the traditional consensus of the Church; we must have a living and vital relationship with God *now*, in the present moment. But in the passion of our current moment with God we often seem in danger of unduly neglecting the vast heft and weight of the past experience and wisdom of millions of fellow Christians. Historian Mark Noll writes perceptively of a variety of Christian "anti-traditionalism" that "privileges one's own current judgments on biblical, theological, and ethical issues (however hastily formed) over insight from the past (however hard won and carefully stated)."[2] In fact, I've heard fellow Christians speak rather contemptuously of what the Christian Church "used to believe" compared to our supposedly more enlightened understanding.

However, the mere passage of time does not guarantee advance in Christian thought and practice. The passage of time could also lead to *regression* if we are not alert. An inheritance is free in one sense, but we still have to work hard to receive it and keep it, and our Christian consensus is just such an inheritance. "It was needful for me to write unto you, and exhort you that you should earnestly contend for the faith which was once delivered unto the saints," Jude reminds us.[3] Even though the Christian deposit has been "delivered" to us, it is still necessary to "earnestly contend" for it; even today, the truths of Christian doctrine must be "hard won and carefully stated," as Noll has it. Otherwise, we might encounter a sort of "theological entropy," in which the passage of time leads to ever-increasing disorder in the Christian faith. The historical consensus of yesterday's Christians serves as a sort of benchmark by which we may measure where we are today.

None of this means that we need to give up on those favorite doctrines of ours. In fact, they may very well be true, and taught by Scripture. The intellectual virtue on the other side of the coin of "humility" is "tenacity," and there is nothing against holding and teaching doctrinal beliefs tenaciously and assuredly, even doctrines outside of those specifically taught in the Creeds. However, my primary argument, the point of this book, is that these doctrines are secondary to those which make us Christians when we believe them and place our faith in Christ. These secondary doctrines should not be used to judge another Christian's spirituality or maturity, or indeed to judge whether or not he or she is truly a Christian after all. Although the Bible contains all manner of worthwhile materials for study and edification, the teachings we engage in our private Bible studies, or even those we hear every week from the pulpits of our local churches, are not the normative equivalent of the accepted doctrines of the Creeds (unless, of course, the accepted doctrines of the Creeds comprise precisely what we are studying and preaching).

In scriptural issues without clear consensus, our attitude should be one of non-judgment; let Christians stand or fall by the judgment of their Master, not by the judgment of fellow believers.[4] In the old saying, let's major on majors and minor on minors.

Questions for Reflection:

1. During a heated debate, Oliver Cromwell once cried out to his opponents, "I beseech ye in the bowels of Christ, think ye that ye may be mistaken!" I am perfectly willing to admit that some of my conclusions in this book may be mistaken. How about you? Are you open to the idea that some of your most sincerely held beliefs

regarding biblical teaching may be mistaken? Which ones in particular?

2.   If a Christian confesses uncertainty on a biblical issue, is that the same thing in your mind as a lack of faith? A lack of wisdom? Why or why not?

3.   Do you have any desire to pursue more extensive studies in the history and heritage of the Christian Church? Why or why not? What might be the value of such a pursuit?

"In Essentials, Unity": A Summary

There's a famous saying from about the year 1625 that has been traced to Lutheran pastor and theologian Peter Meiderlin: "We would be in the best shape if we kept in essentials, Unity; in non-essentials, Liberty; and in both Charity." In fact, this saying has become so well known among German Christian writers, they "have coined a special term" for it: "They call it the *Friedensspruch* or 'Peace Saying.'"[5]

Not only did Meiderlin live during the time of the Thirty Years' War between the Habsburgs and their numerous enemies, but he also endured a great deal of post-Reformation strife between competing Christian factions. On the one hand, Lutheran and Calvinist groups disputed over how best to preserve the "authentic" Protestant heritage as embodied in Lutheranism; on the other, Roman Catholics disputed over how best to rebut Protestantism and promote the interests of the Catholic Church. It is no wonder that many began crying out for peace.

Among those seeking peace and unity was Meiderlin, who first wrote his famous sentence (under his Latinate name Rupertus Meldenius) in the book *A Prayerful Admonition for Peace to the Theologians of the Augsburg Confession.*[6] Hans Rollmann summarizes the opening of this book:

Peter Meiderlin's argument for peace in the church starts out with a story about a dream he had. In it he encounters a devout Christian theologian in a white robe sitting at a table and reading the Scriptures. All of a sudden Christ appears to him as the victor over death and the devil, warns him of an impending danger, and admonishes him to be very vigilant. Then Christ vanishes and the Devil appears in the form of a blinding light, moonlight to be exact, and claims to have been sent on a mission from God. He states that in this final age the Church needs to be protected from all heresy and apostasy of any kind and God's elect have the duty to safeguard and keep pure the doctrinal truths they inherited. The devil then alleges that God has authorized him to found a new order of these doctrinally pure elect, some sort of a doctrinal heritage coven. Those who join will bind themselves to an oath of strictest observance to these doctrines. The devil then extends to our devout theologian the invitation to join this militant fellowship for his own eternal welfare. Our theologian thinks about what he has just heard and decides to bring it in prayer before God, upon which the devil immediately vanishes and Christ reappears. Christ tenderly raises the trembling Christian up, comforts him most kindly, and before he departs admonishes him to remain loyal only to the Word of God in simplicity and humility of heart. For Meldenius, this dream depicted in a powerful way the state of his own church, and the resultant admonition is his own contribution on how to keep the peace.[7]

In other words, Meiderlin sees the quest for uniform doctrinal purity, with its underlying methods of "heresy hunting" and factional hair-splitting, as a temptation from the Devil, who appears as the emissary of righteousness, an "angel of light."[8] Although "unity" in essentials is necessary for the peace of the Christian body, so also is "liberty" in non-essentials—and above all Christians must maintain love, or "charity," in all matters. As Meiderlin argues later, Christian peace and love strengthen even the weak elements of the church, while the lack of these will bring down even the greatest and most powerful.

> Does that mean that there is no need for doctrines? Certainly not. But only those doctrinal statements are necessary that center on salvation, follow unmistakably Scripture, have been formulated in universal confessional statements, and are considered true by the great majority of believing theologians. The insistence of belief in theological minutiae or non-essentials is in the mind of the author [Meiderlin] only designed to destroy Christianity itself.[9]

On the other hand, some might argue that in matters of faith there is no such thing as a non-essential. Such was the viewpoint of second-generation Lutheran and acquaintance of Luther himself, Matthias Flacius, against whom Meiderlin was at least in part reacting. Described as "the ablest and most uncompromising of the ultra-Lutherans" and as "always sincere if not always dispassionate," Flacius saw himself as a figure holding to the purity of biblical Christianity, standing at times alone against the "compromising" tendencies of other Protestant Christians such as Melanchthon. In the words of one historian, "He had the faults of his qualities, and it is sometimes difficult to distinguish his zeal from fanaticism, his firmness from intolerance."[10] In some matters his views carried the day; in others they did not. Melanchthon himself wrote to Flacius at one point, offering to apologize publicly over one of their doctrinal divisions if only for the sake of unity (even though Melanchthon had previously called Flacius a "viper"). However, whether on the winning side or the losing, in all matters Flacius continually engaged himself in controversy for the sake of the right understanding of the Scriptures as he interpreted them.

I bring up both Meiderlin and Flacius in order to reach a question for you to ponder: In today's Christian world, are we better served by the example of Meiderlin or the example of Flacius? Is it better to stand for a united body in the area of essentials, allowing liberty in non-essentials, or is it better to strive for exactitude in all matters, even if that exactitude leads to narrower and narrower factionalism?

This is not a rhetorical question. Many today do seem to think the greatest need of the Christian church is for a more or less complete and seamless doctrinal purity, free of all "heresy" as they see it, and they are willing to engage in controversy for however long it takes until their opponents admit their errors and retire from the battlefield. Others (like myself) do not think the true Christian church should be viewed as a battlefield *at all*—especially when the opposing sides are both made up of faithful Christians. Our only battles should be against the spiritual works of darkness, not against those fellow members of the Body of Christ with whom we may have relatively minor disagreements.

"A unifying vision of the church may seem to be a pipe dream," theology professor Roger Olson writes in his book *The Mosaic of Christian Belief*, "but in reality it need not be that. In spite of continuing debates between theologians and church officers, the laity (ordinary church members) are already forging ahead with visible, if not institutional, unity of the church." Olson goes on to say:

> Perhaps the time has come for denominational Christian leaders to catch up with the practice of their laypeople and drop the barriers to full fellowship that have stood so long in the way of the church's unity.[11]

In this book, what I've argued is that many of these "barriers to full fellowship" are the doctrines which actually are not essential elements of Christian belief. Thus, even if one group holds and preaches them as perfectly legitimate doctrines, other equally faithful Christians may not, without thereby necessitating a rupture in fellowship or unity between the differing groups.

Once again, what are these issues I've referred to as "non-essential" and "secondary"? What is it believers don't have to believe? Here's a summary of them, the basic issues covered so far:

What Christians should believe about Creation: God exists and is the cause of all things that truly exist. God is the Creator of the universe and its contents.

What you don't have to believe: God created all things in six literal 24-hour days, roughly 6,000 years ago. *There are other, equally scriptural, interpretations of Creation.*

What Christians should believe about the Bible: The Bible is God's inspired Word, infallibly true in all it contains and inerrant if read in the way its divine Author intends it to be read.

What you don't have to believe: Every part of the Bible is intended to be read as literal history; all parts of the Bible are equally historical. *There are other, equally scriptural, interpretations of how to read the Bible.*

What Christians should believe about humans: Humans are fallen and sinful, and require the salvation brought about by God's grace through faith in Christ.

What you don't have to believe: Humans are so corrupted and depraved by the Fall they possess neither freedom of will nor trustworthy rational faculties. *There are other, equally scriptural, interpretations of the human condition.*

What Christians should believe about involvement in politics: Christians should be involved in their political order as the times require and dictate, whether to reform institutions and extend liberties as far as possible, or to preserve the often fragile liberties, freedoms, and institutions already possessed.

What you don't have to believe: Except in extreme cases (e.g., takeover of a country by an evil dictatorship), a person's Christian faith is not to be judged based on membership in any particular political party. Political movements rarely possess any sort of Christian monopoly in either vice or virtue. *There are other, equally scriptural, interpretations of what Christian involvement in politics requires.*

What Christians should believe about the end times: Jesus is Lord over all the earth and all creation, both spiritual and physical. There will be a final Resurrection of the dead and a final Judgment, after which will come eternity in which all humans will be either with God or apart from Him.

What you don't have to believe: There will be a Rapture or catching away, in which millions of believers will disappear to go with Christ to Heaven, while the rest of the world's population is "left behind." There follows a seven-year Tribulation during which a literal Antichrist will rise to rule the earth; after this Jesus will come to the valley of Armageddon for a climactic world battle, followed by a thousand years of earthly peace in which raptured believers return to earth to rule over non-raptured humans. This thousand years of peace will be followed by the release of Satan to tempt the earth once more, followed by a final Judgment. Satan will be thrown into eternal torment, and God will create a literal new heavens and new earth in which the saved will dwell forever. *There are other, equally scriptural, interpretations of end-time events.*

Now let's examine your acceptance or non-acceptance of these conclusions. I'd like you to go back through this list, especially focusing on the second half of each issue raised. Rate your level of agreement with my "What you don't have to believe" conclusions, on a scale of 1 through 5:

5 = I completely agree with the conclusion. This belief is not really essential to hold in order for one to qualify as a Bible-believing Christian.
4 = I agree somewhat with the conclusion.
3 = I am unsure whether or not I agree with the conclusion.
2 = I disagree somewhat with the conclusion.
1 = I completely disagree with the conclusion. This belief really is essential to hold in order for one to qualify as a Bible-believing Christian.

Now add together all five of your scores. Here's what your total could mean:

18-25—You are in substantial agreement with much of this book.
14-17—You are unsure of whether or not you agree with this book.
5-13—You are in substantial disagreement with much of this book.

I wonder: Where would Peter Meiderlin and Matthias Flacius fall in this ranking?

Questions for Reflection:

1. What were your scores? With how much of this book did you completely agree? Somewhat agree? Somewhat disagree? Completely disagree? With how much were you unsure?

2. Did any of the discussions of these issues in previous chapters cause you to become angry? What do you think of Christians who become angry over interpretive disputes? Did the book seem deliberately provocative?

3. Despite my oft-stated concern for unity among Christians, did this book strike you as being too divisive or controversial to be of benefit? Why or why not?

4. Have you changed your mind on any of the issues raised? Which ones? Are you more confirmed than ever in your beliefs on certain issues? Which ones? Why?

5. "Finally, brethren, farewell. Be perfect, be of good comfort, be of one mind, live in peace; and the God of love and peace shall be with you. . . . The grace of the Lord Jesus Christ, and the love of God, and the communion of the Holy Ghost, be with you all. Amen."[12] Whether we consider ourselves a Peter Meiderlin or a Matthias Flacius, may we "be of one mind" and "live in peace." In all things may you and I have charity, the bond of perfectness,[13] for

you are my brothers and sisters in the Lord, a part of my family under Christ. (Of course, you know the corollary to this: It means I'm part of *your* family, too.)

References

1) Richard John Neuhaus, "The Public Square." *First Things* Feb. 1994: 57.

2) Mark Noll, "The Evangelical Mind Today." *First Things* Oct. 2004: 34.

3) Jude 3.

4) Romans 14:4.

5) Hans Rollmann, "In Essentials Unity: The Pre-History and History of a Restoration Movement Slogan." Lecture given at "Christian Scholars Conference," July 1996. David Lipscomb University, Nashville, Tennessee. Reprinted at believersweb.org.

6) For a summary of Meiderlin's book in English, see John Benjamin Rust, *The Great Peace Motto.* Cleveland: Central Publishing House, 1929.

7) Hans Rollmann, "In Essentials Unity."

8) 2 Cor. 11:14.

9) Hans Rollmann, "In Essentials Unity."

10) James Strahan, "Flacius." *Encyclopedia of Religion and Ethics, Volume 6.* Edited by James Hastings, John A. Selbie, and Louis H. Gray. New York and Edinburgh: Charles Scribner's Sons and T. & T. Clark, 1914: 48-49.

11) Roger E. Olson, *The Mosaic of Christian Belief: Twenty Centuries of Unity and Diversity.* Downers Grove, Illinois: InterVarsity Press, 2002: 305.

12) 2 Cor. 13:11, 14.

13) Col. 3:14.

Chapter 9: Grace and Peace to You

"Now I beseech you, brethren, by the name of our Lord Jesus Christ, that you all speak the same thing, and that there be no divisions among you; but that you be perfectly joined together in the same mind and in the same judgment."—1 Cor. 1:10.

"One man esteemeth one day above another: another esteemeth every day alike. Let every man be fully persuaded in his own mind. . . . Let us therefore follow after the things which make for peace, and things wherewith one may edify another."—Romans 14:5, 19.

Second-Class Christians

Isn't it odd that the same person wrote the two scriptural passages quoted above? On the one hand, Paul the apostle begs the Corinthian church to "speak the same thing," to have "no divisions," and to be "perfectly joined together in the same mind and in the same judgment." He seems to be asking the Corinthians for a perfected doctrinal and confessional unity. On the other hand, the same author spends an entire chapter in his Epistle to the Romans commanding the Roman church to avoid "doubtful disputations" in their teaching (14:1); he tells them not to judge their fellow Christians in matters of belief, for "Who art thou that judgest another man's servant? to his own master he standeth or falleth" (vs. 4); he instructs them as a body, "Let every man be fully persuaded in his own mind" as to matters of religious observance (vs. 5). Doesn't Paul seem to demand unity of belief and practice out of the Corinthian church while allowing liberty of belief and practice to the Roman church?

By now you probably can predict the moral I intend to draw here. There is no real mystery to Paul's apparent inconsistency once we realize that our walk of love in the Body of Christ requires unity in the *essential* beliefs and liberty in the *non-essentials*. Writing to the Corinthians, Paul has to deal with essential issues such as whether or not Christ actually rose from the dead, right Christian conduct in sexual matters, and so on; writing to the Romans, the essentials for the most part seem to be in place, but Paul has to salve a disagreement between some who eat sacrificial meat and some who do not (this discussion arises in the Corinthian letter as well). To the Corinthians, Paul prescribes unity, to the

Romans liberty. As we saw in the last chapter, "We would be in the best shape if we kept in essentials, Unity; in non-essentials, Liberty; and in both Charity."

However, it's so often the little foxes that spoil the vine[1]; it's the non-essentials that incessantly cause us to lose our charitable acceptance of one another in Christ. As John Wesley points out, right opinions of God and biblical doctrine may exist in a person who has not one right love either toward God or toward Christ's Church.[2] Ninety percent of our arguments with fellow Christian groups and individuals are not ten percent as important as we think they are at the time. Even in the early church, we see the same problem arising:

> And in those days, when the number of the disciples was multiplied, there arose a murmuring of the Grecians against the Hebrews, because their widows were neglected in the daily ministration.[3]

The Hebraic Christians in Jerusalem, who understood Greek but also as Jews spoke Hebrew and read the Hebrew Bible, had sold much property and were using the money to help take care of the needy among them. The Hellenistic Christians, here called the "Grecians," who were also Jewish converts but who spoke and read only Greek, quickly began to notice discrimination on the part of the Hebraic believers against them.

In his commentary on the Book of Acts, Richard Longenecker relates the following regarding this passage: "According to the Talmud, Pharisaism made little secret of its contempt for Hellenists and . . . they were frequently categorized by the native-born and assumedly more scrupulous populace of Jerusalem as second-class Israelites." Even after the Hebraic Jews had become Christians, "it appears that this attitude of Hebraic superiority was rather widespread."[4] Moreover, this superiority was not based on "linguistic or geographic considerations alone," but also "intellectual orientation"—in other words, the assumed superiority of the Hebraic Christians over the Hellenists at least partially was based on their supposedly superior doctrinal understanding.

Earlier commentators from the 1800s had similar insights. For instance, J.B. Lightfoot in his *Commentary from the Talmud* argues, "Grant that it [the Greek language] were in some esteem among them [the Hebraic Jews], because, indeed, most of the learned Rabbins did understand it; yet what account must they make of those Jews that knew no other language but the Greek? Surely they must be looked upon as in the lower, yes, the lowest degree of Jews, who were such strangers to the language so peculiar to that nation, that is, the Hebrew."[5]

So early on we see factionalism developing within the Church over relatively minor causes; in fact, we see the development of "second-class Christians" receiving second-class treatment. Of necessity, the existence of "second-class Christians" entails the existence as well of "first-class" Christians, those whose attitude of superiority is based on a different "intellectual orientation" than that of the "second-class" group. "They might call themselves Christians," this attitude seems to say, "but they certainly don't deserve the same treatment or consideration that we *real* Christians do."

In the Introduction to this book, I wrote the following:

Virtually all [Christian] groups mentioned would maintain that they themselves *are* securely founded in the Bible, and that their beliefs and practices are grounded in God's Word. However, at the same time many of those groups would further maintain that many of the other groups *are not* so founded—that, in fact, many of the others might be Christians in the sense of having Jesus as their Lord, but they are surely second-class Christians (or even third-class) in the sense of not really believing and / or practicing the biblical essentials of the Christian faith.

Of course, this attitude does not seem to be anything new under the sun. Throughout the New Testament, Paul the apostle and other spiritual leaders have to deal almost continually with one manifestation or another of factionalist "party spirit." Here are a few examples:[6]

- Paul tells the Galatians that factionalism is a "work of the flesh" and that "There is neither Jew nor Greek, there is neither bond nor free, there is neither male nor female: for ye are all one in Christ Jesus."[7]
- He rebukes the Corinthians: "For ye are yet carnal: for whereas there is among you envying, and strife, and divisions, are ye not carnal, and walk as [mere] men? For while one saith, I am of Paul; and another, I am of Apollos; are ye not carnal?"[8]
- He warns the Romans: "Mark them which cause divisions."[9]
- He prepares Timothy as a pastor: "Foolish and unlearned questions avoid, knowing that they do gender strifes. And the servant of the Lord must not strive"; he also tells Timothy to charge others that they "strive not about words to no profit," because from "strifes of words" come "envy, strife, railings."[10]
- He tells Titus to avoid "contentions and strivings about the law."[11]
- In the Book of Acts, Paul confronts "certain of the sect of the Pharisees which believed,"[12] who came in "to spy out our liberty which we have in Christ Jesus, that they might bring us into bondage"[13] (by requiring legalistic, unnecessary observances brought in from the Jewish Law. To the Pharisaical Christians, these ritual observances apparently promoted one from the "second class" of Christianity to the "first").
- During the period of this confrontation, Paul also challenges and rebukes Peter himself: "For before that certain came from James, he did eat with the Gentiles: but when they were come, he withdrew himself and separated himself, fearing them which were of the circumcision."[14] In other words, Peter associated with the "second-class" Christians until members of the "first-class" group

showed up, at which time he remembered his Hebraic status and segregated himself.

And these are only a few of the passages involving strife and factionalism in the early church! However, despite all these potential divisions, Paul perseveres in his relentless message of the love and unity of the true Christian Body: "Now in Christ Jesus ye who sometimes were far off are made nigh by the blood of Christ. For He is our peace, who hath made both [Jewish and Gentile Christians] one, and hath broken down the middle wall of partition between us."[15]

In fact, in his characteristically charitable style, Paul finds a way to greet all Christians as equals, with what we might call his "signature" salutation. The Book of Ephesians furnishes a typical example of that which shows up in all of Paul's letters:

> Grace be to you, and peace, from God our Father, and from the Lord Jesus Christ.[16]

"Peace" (the Greek *eirene*, translating the Hebrew *shalom*) was (and still is) both the greeting and the farewell commonly used by the Jews, even as *aloha* is used in Hawaii today. The Greeks used "grace" (*charis*) in exactly the same fashion; therefore, when Paul uses "grace and peace" as his salutation, he is greeting Gentile and Jewish Christians alike, placing them upon a perfectly equal footing:

> The phrases which open the epistles of Paul are of deep import. It is true that they follow the forms with which, in his day, letters usually were begun. Yet they never are empty formulas. . . . "Grace" was a familiar salutation among the Greeks; "peace," a usual greeting among Jews; both have been united and filled with a new glory by Christians. Paul's salutation was a prayer. It well may be our petition for one another and for ourselves.[17]

"Paul's salutation was a prayer" in the sense that he is praying not only for Christians to receive God's "grace" and therefore God's "peace" as well— rather, his use of the two terms together implies also a prayer for the unity of all Christians, no matter their background or current status. Thus, in the opening to every one of his epistles, Paul seeks to erase the "first class / second class" distinction so regrettably prevalent even among members of the same Body.

I am not saying there are no differences in faith, understanding, knowledge, or maturity among Christians; that would be a ridiculous assertion.

However, I *am* saying that the tendency on the part of so many of us to compare ourselves to others and to measure others' levels of biblical "spirituality" is itself unbiblical and a sign of spiritual immaturity. When Paul writes of those who "commend themselves" by "measuring themselves by themselves, and comparing themselves among themselves," he concludes they "are not wise."[18] In Christ there is no "second class," and at least in theory we all know that quite well.

So why should we continue to treat fellow believers as if there were?

Questions for Reflection:

1. Earlier in this section I wrote, "Ninety percent of our arguments with fellow Christian groups and individuals are not ten percent as important as we think they are at the time." Of course, this opinion is just based on my observation, not on any kind of scientific survey. So what do you think? Does it seem accurate?

2. If you do think the above quoted sentence is accurate, how might your attitudes and behavior change in the future when disagreements arise between you and other Christians?

3. I mentioned the terms "first class" and "second class" with regard to Christians. Allow me to repeat those terms here: "first-class Christians" / "second-class Christians." Now: What groups of people immediately pop into your mind as fitting these categories?

4. Why those particular groups?

The Knowledge of Christ

This book easily could have been twice as long as it is. Just think of all the other topics that could have been addressed but weren't:

- Whether or not Christians are biblically required to tithe their incomes.
- What day of the week is to be considered the Sabbath day.
- Whether or not Christians are biblically required even to *observe* a Sabbath day.
- Whether or not there is a biblically exact method of baptism.
- What style or practice of Communion we should observe.
- Whether or not the King James Version is the "chosen" English translation of the Bible.
- The meaning of the Pentecostal / charismatic experience today (the role of glossolalia, the ministry of spiritual gifts, healing and the miraculous, the Holy Spirit's presence in the life of a believer, etc.).
- Whether or not the stories of the "fall of Lucifer" are biblically warranted.

- Whether or not Christians can "lose" their salvation through unbelief or neglect.
- The role of denominationalism within Christianity.
- The question of how much Christians in their daily lives should live within and how far they should accommodate themselves to the culture around them—i.e., the question of how "separate" Christians should be "from" the world while living "within" the world.
- The question of male / female and husband / wife relationships within the Church.
- The questions surrounding worship styles (music choices, liturgical services vs. non-liturgical, the level and type of congregational involvement, etc.).
- Whether or not salvation through Christ might extend in the world beyond the number of those who are actively professing Christians.
- The wide variety of other questions involving Christian attitudes toward money and prosperity; war and national conflicts; capital punishment and other legal issues; welfare aid to the poor; divorce and re-marriage.
- And so on.

However, I think enough issues have been covered for us to bring out the point: What is it that believers don't have to believe? What is it one can *not* believe and still be a faithful, biblically-oriented Christian? And why is the attitude so prevalent that Christians who do not believe exactly as we do are somehow "second-class" believers?

It is my sincere prayer that the consideration of these questions, and our tentative answers to them, will help to unite the true Christian Church. I prize doctrinal exactitude above most things; however, I prize faith, hope, and love even more highly. "Underlying the numerous Christian visions of the true nature of the church and its visible, organizational structure and the sacraments is a basic, bedrock unity of belief: the church is the people of God, founded by Christ Himself to be the community of the Holy Spirit and the anticipation of his future kingdom," writes one theologian. He goes on later:

> Almost without doubt significant differences of understanding of these realities will remain among Christians until history ends. But Christians can return to their basic, underlying agreement about the church and use it as common ground for mutual understanding, respect, and cooperation for mission and service.[19]

As Jesus Himself teaches, the world will believe in Christ and his salvific mission, not when they perceive our doctrinal exactitude, but when they see that we are one.[20]

Perhaps the very concept of "mere" Christianity seems too thin or too basic to you. Or you might think that the "mature" Christian should grow past these basics and into the other beliefs discussed. However, let's remember what was said by Karl Barth, one of the twentieth century's leading theologians, when someone asked him to relate the most important knowledge he had gained during his lifetime of study. Barth pondered for a moment before replying: "Jesus loves me, this I know, for the Bible tells me so." This is the all-important foundation, never to be altered.[21]

The basics are never merely basic; the knowledge of Christ is never too "thin" for further reflection. What Christian believers *should* believe is far more important than what they don't have to believe. "In Him we live and move and have our being."[22] We all can agree at least on that.

References

1) Song of Solomon 2:15.

2) As quoted in A.W. Tozer, *The Pursuit of God*. Orig. pub. 1949. Camp Hill, Pennsylvania: Christian Publications, 1993: 8-9.

3) Acts 6:1.

4) Richard N. Longenecker, "The Acts of the Apostles." In *The Expositor's Bible Commentary, Volume 9*. Edited by Frank E. Gaebelein. Grand Rapids, Michigan: Zondervan, 1981: 329.

5) J.B. Lightfoot, "Exercitations upon the Acts." In *A Commentary upon the New Testament from the Talmud and Hebraica, Volume 4*. Orig. pub. 1859. Grand Rapids, Michigan: Baker Book House, 1979: 60-61.

6) Many of the following examples are paraphrased from A. Colin Day, *Roget's Thesaurus of the Bible*. Edison, New Jersey: Castle Books, 2003.

7) Galatians 3:28, 5:20.

8) 1 Cor. 3:3-4.

9) Romans 16:17.

10) 2 Timothy 2:23-24; 2:14; 1 Timothy 6:4.

11) Titus 3:9.

12) Acts 15:5.

13) Galatians 2:4.

14) Galatians 2:12.

15) Ephesians 2:13-14.

16) Ephesians 1:2.

17) Charles R. Erdman, *The First Epistle of Paul to the Corinthians: An Exposition.* 5th printing. Philadelphia: The Westminster Press, 1976: 21, 24.

18) 2 Cor. 10:12.

19) Roger E. Olson, *The Mosaic of Christian Belief: Twenty Centuries of Unity and Diversity.* Downers Grove, Illinois: InterVarsity Press, 2002: 303.

20) John 17:21-23.

21) 1 Cor. 3:11.

22) Acts 17:28.

Index

Second Coming, the, 57-58, 115, 119,
    122, 129
Seneca, 141
Shermer, Michael, 34, 36
Smith, Larry T., 136n24
Socrates, vii, 41, 75-76
Spong, John Shelby, 100
Spurgeon, Charles, 4-5, 122
"Symbolist" interpretation, 119, 122-23
Tacelli, Ronald, 61, 67
Tacitus, 64
Tertullian, 11, 13
Thomas Aquinas
    See Aquinas, Thomas
Tinder, Glenn, 104-6
Titus, 126-27, 129
Tolkien, J.R.R., 71, 75

"total depravity," x, 78-82
Trent, Council of, 84
Trinity, 8-9, 16
VanderLugt, Herbert, 118
Vincent of Lérins, 5-11, 14-18, 142
Voegelin, Eric, 68
Walvoord, John, 132
Weinberg, Steven, 40
Wesley, John, 152
Whisenant, Edgar, 116
Whithrow, G.J., 36
Wilson, John, 28
Wycliffe, John, 122
Yancey, Philip, 111
Zalman, Rabbi Elijah ben Solomon
    See Gaon, Vilna
Zwingli, Ulrich, 122

About the author

Craig Payne teaches at Indian Hills Community College in southeastern Iowa, where he lives with his wife, Desirae, and children, Nathan and Erin. Holding degrees in both literature and philosophy, he has published many articles and poems in various journals, and has won six writing awards in the annual Amy Foundation competitions. His previous books are *The Washing of the Word* (Xulon Press, 2002) and *Where Myth and History Meet: A Christian Response to Myth* (University Press of America, 2001).